Fabulous
Fruit
Cooking

FABULOUS FRUIT COOKING

*A Gourmet Guide
to Great Fruit Dishes
from Soup to Sorbet*

Andreas Miessmer

Lark Books

Editor: Deborah Morgenthal
Editorial Assistant: Laura Dover
Art Direction and Production: Celia Naranjo
Photographer: cover and pages 4, 6. 15–16 (cranberries), 17 (left), 19 (bottom),
  22-23 (bottom), 25, (mango), 28 (bottom), 29 (nectarine), 30, 35, 38-39 (bottom center),
  41-42 (raspberries), and 43 (bottom) Evan Bracken; page 5, 8, 10, 13-14 (cherries), and 37
  (plums), Richard Babb

Library of Congress Cataloging-in-Publication Data
Miessmer, Andreas.
      Fabulous fruit cooking: a gourmet guide to great fruit dishes
    from soup to sorbet / Andreas Miessmer.
            p.   cm.
      Includes index.
      ISBN 1-887374-07-8
      1. Cookery (Fruit)   I. Title.
    TX811.M49   1996
    641.6'4--dc20   96-4215
                                               CIP

10 9 8 7 6 5 4 3 2 1

Published in 1996 by Lark Books
Altamont Press
50 College Street
Asheville, NC 28801

Distributed in the U.S. by Sterling Publishing, 387 Park Avenue. South,
  New York, NY 10016; 1-800-367-9692
Distributed in Canada by Sterling Publishing, c/o Canadian Manda Group,
  One Atlantic Avenue, Suite 105, Toronto, Ontario, Canada M6K 3E7
Distributed in Great Britain and Europe by Cassell PLC, Wellington House,
  125 Strand, London, England WC2R OBB
Distributed in Australia by Capricorn Link (Australia) Pty Ltd., P.O. Box 6651,
  Baulkham Hills, Business Center, New South Wales 2153

Every effort has been made to ensure that all the information in this book is accurate.
However, due to differing conditions, tools, and individual skills, the publisher cannot be
responsible for any injuries, losses, and other damages which may result from the use of the
information in this book.

Printed in Hong Kong

ISBN 0-887374-07-8

Table of Contents

Preface 6

Fruit Basics
Apple .7
Apricot 8
Avocado 9
Banana 10
Blueberry 10
Cactus Pear 11
Cape Gooseberry 12
Cherimoya 12
Cherry 13
Coconut 14
Cranberry 15
Currant 16
Date .17
Fig 18
Grape 19
Grapefruit 20
Guava 21
Kiwi .22
Kumquat 31
Lemon 22
Lime .23
Loquat 24
Lychee 24
Mango 25
Mangosteen 26
Melon 27
Nashi 29

Nectarine 29
Orange 30
Papaya 32
Passion Fruit 33
Peach 34
Pear 35
Persimmon 35
Pineapple 36
Plum .37
Pomegranate 38
Pomelo 39
Quince 40
Rambutan 41
Star Fruit 42
Strawberry 43
Tamarillo 43
Tangerine 44
Watermelon 45

Recipe Basics 46

Appetizers and Soups 48
Poultry and Meat 66
Seafood 86
Pastries 106
Desserts 122

Recipes by Fruit 141
Recipe Index 142

Why, of all books, a fruit cookbook? This question is justified, considering the large number of cookbooks that have been published on this subject. Through improved transport and cooling methods, the supply of fruits from domestic and foreign producers is growing rapidly. Because of the increasing availability of exotic fruits (which is our focus in this book), questions often arise concerning proper preparation.

As an experienced gourmet cook, this subject interests me greatly. On trips, in markets, as well as through a study of international cuisine, I have become acquainted with the fruit kitchen. I believe I can offer you basic information that will help you prepare delicious recipes using a wide assortment of beautiful and tasty fruits from around the world.

I will first introduce you to the individual types of fruit in the chapter "Fruit Basics." Here, each fruit is described in detail, and tips regarding their purchase, storage, and preparation are provided. These tips are easy to follow.

The rest of the book is devoted to 85 superb recipes featuring fruit. Unfortunately, I can present you only with a selection of my favorite recipes from my kitchen, because a book could be written about cooking with berries and citrus fruits alone. Now let me welcome you to the kitchen of aromatic and exotic fruits. I wish you much success and many delectable dining experiences.

Andreas Miessmer

Apple

ORIGIN

The apple is one of the oldest and most widely eaten fruits in the world. It originated in Central Asia and today boasts over 20,000 varieties worldwide. In the United States, apples are grown commercially in thirty-five states, primarily in Washington and New York.

DESCRIPTION AND TASTE

Apples are divided into eating and cooking apples. The taste ranges from very sour to very sweet, and the pulp can be crunchy, hard, or mealy. Some common varieties are Cox's Orange Pippin, Cortland, Golden Delicious, Red Delicious, Granny Smith, Jonathon, McIntosh, Gravenstein, and Winesap.

PURCHASE AND STORAGE

Because they come in such a wide variety, and because they keep so well, apples are available throughout the year. Only cooking apples of high quality should be used in recipes. Depending on the variety, apples can be stored for up to six weeks in the refrigerator. They will go bad quickly at room temperature, but can be frozen without hesitation.

CHARACTERISTICS

Apples have a high nutritional value; they are a good source of fiber and their peels are very rich in pectin. The pulp contains organic acids, several kinds of sugars, cellulose, tannins, and more than 20 vitamins and minerals. Peeled apples turn brown quickly, so lemon juice should be sprinkled over them as soon as possible.

TIPS ON HOW TO USE

While apples were originally used primarily for their juice, today they are well suited to a wide range of dishes. In particular, they are excellent in a wide variety of desserts, stewed fruits, sauces, jellies, wines, or brandy. Apples also combine nicely with vegetables and meat dishes (especially pork).

PREPARATION

1. Thinly peel the apple.

2. For slices, core the apple with an apple corer or a small knife, then cut the fruit into slices.

3. For pieces, cut out the core with a small knife, then cut the fruit into pieces.

Apricot

ORIGIN

The apricot originated in China at the time of Alexander the Great, about 330 B.C. Today, most apricots come from the Mediterranean countries, Hungary, Israel, California, and Washington.

DESCRIPTION AND TASTE

Apricots are stone fruits and are related to plums. They are usually about the size of a large ice cream scoop. The velvety-to-rough skin is light yellow or orange and has a lovely fragrance. The light orange flesh of the ripe apricot is delicate, juicy, and extraordinarily delicious.

The stones of the apricots are used like almonds, as they also contain prussic acid.

PURCHASE AND STORAGE

The peak season for apricots is July and August, though those grown in California and Washington are also available in May and June. In the winter months, some are imported from the Southern Hemisphere. Ripe apricots last only a couple of days.

TIPS ON HOW TO USE

Apricots can be used in many ways and combined with numerous foods. They are often used in baking and cooking recipes.

PREPARATION

1. Cut around the fruit in the direction of the seam; turn the two halves, break the fruit open, and remove the stone.

2. To remove the skin, cut into the skin crosswise, dip the fruit for five to ten seconds in boiling water, then chill. Pull off the skin with a knife.

2. Take out the stone with the tip of a knife. Immediately trickle lemon juice on the pulp to prevent it from turning brown.

3. Spoon the pulp directly out of the skin.

Avocado

ORIGIN

The large, evergreen avocado tree originated in the tropics of Central America. Today, the most important avocado-growing countries are Mexico, the United States, the West Indies, Brazil, Indonesia, South Africa, Peru, Kenya, Australia, Spain, and Israel.

DESCRIPTION AND TASTE

The avocado is a pear-shaped stone fruit that can be green, reddish, or almost black. The texture of the skin can vary from rough and scarred to quite smooth. The fruit weighs from $\frac{1}{2}$ to 1 pound (230 to 454 g). The light green-to-yellow, soft, buttery pulp tastes slightly sweet and nutty and encloses an inedible dark brown stone.

PURCHASE AND STORAGE

A fully ripe avocado is soft and the skin dents when slightly pressed with the finger. Ripe fruits can be stored a day or two in the refrigerator, but are sensitive to pressure and can easily develop brown spots. Unripe fruits ripen at room temperature in one to three days.

CHARACTERISTICS

In contrast to other fruits, avocados contain a lot of fat (about 30%). Trickle lemon juice on avocados that have been cut to prevent their turning brown.

TIPS ON HOW TO USE

Because of its mild flavor, the avocado works well in combination with a variety of foods. But its suitability for cooking is limited because the pulp turns slightly bitter when heated.

PREPARATION

1. Cut the avocado lengthwise up to the stone. Then twist the two halves in opposite directions, and detach them from each other.

4. If you need slices, peel the halved fruit with a peeler, and cut it into slices.

Banana

ORIGIN

Besides the apple, the banana is the most common fruit. One of the oldest cultivated fruits, it originated in Southeast Asia. The regions where it is primarily grown are South and Central America, Africa, the Canaries, and the West Indies. Bananas are not grown in the United States, except for a small crop in Hawaii.

DESCRIPTION AND TASTE

Bananas are divided into eating or yellow bananas, cooking bananas (plantain), red bananas, and Lady Finger (miniature) bananas. Yellow bananas represent by far the largest share of the banana market. Bananas are harvested while unripe, when the skin is still green. When ripe, they are bright yellow and the pulp is soft, light-colored, and tastes sweet and mild.

PURCHASE AND STORAGE

Bananas can be bought, without hesitation, while they are still unripe, because they ripen quickly at room temperature. Small black spots appear on the skin when the fruit is overripe. When this occurs, the fruit should be eaten immediately. Bananas are very sensitive to pressure, and they should not be stored in the refrigerator, because the flavor gets lost, and the fruit goes bad quickly.

CHARACTERISTICS

Peeled bananas turn brown quickly. In order to avoid this, you should trickle some lemon juice on the fruit when it has been peeled.

TIPS ON HOW TO USE

The banana can be used for desserts, ice cream, salads, curries, and much more.

PREPARATION

There is no need for a detailed explanation of how to prepare a banana, since the technique has been known to the majority of us since we were children.

Blueberry

ORIGIN

Blueberries are native to the northern areas of the Northern Hemisphere and were a staple of Native Americans before the arrival of the explorers.

DESCRIPTION AND TASTE

Blueberries are black or blue and are about the size of a pea. They are juicy and sweet, with a slightly bitter aftertaste. The pulp is lighter than the skin and contains edible pits.

PURCHASE AND STORAGE

Blueberries are in season from May to September, though they are at their peak in June, July, and August. The berries are sensitive to pressure and go bad very quickly. They can be stored for a short time only and are best spread out flat on a cloth in a cool place. They can also be easily frozen.

CHARACTERISTICS

The berries are rich in fruit acids, vitamins A, B, and C, tannic acids, and minerals, especially iron. The juice causes stains, which, due to their high content of tannic acids, are hard to remove.

TIPS ON HOW TO USE

Blueberries are eaten fresh, with sugar or yogurt, or they are processed to make marmalade, stewed fruits, wine, liqueur, and brandy. In addition, they are commonly used in baking.

PREPARATION

Wash the berries and, if necessary, remove the leaves and the stems. Let the berries dry on a cloth.

Cactus Pear

ORIGIN

There are numerous cacti, all of which are of the Opuntia variety, whose fruits are eaten. The cactus pear, also called the prickly pear, tuna, indian fig, and indian pear, originated in Mexico. It has now spread over most tropical and subtropical countries. It is grown primarily in Southern California, Central and South America, Australia, South Africa, Algeria, Tunisia, Egypt, Israel, and in some Mediterranean countries.

DESCRIPTION AND TASTE

The Opuntia grows up to 13 feet high (4 m). After some years, it produces yellow blossoms at the edges of its limbs, which eventually develop into fruit. The fruits are 1½ to 4 inches long (4 to 10 cm), egg-shaped, and slightly flattened. They have bulges on their skin, which are covered in small, thin, very sharp needles. Unripe fruits are green. The skin changes color with increasing degrees of ripeness from yellow to orange to brown. The yellow-red pulp is jellylike, juicy, tastes refreshingly sweet, and contains many small edible seed pits.

PURCHASE AND STORAGE

Look for cactus pears from fall through spring and occasionally during summer months. Since the fruits are not easily transported, they are packed individually in paper or in crates with dividers. Before cactus pears are put on the market, most of the needles are brushed off. They can be stored in the refrigerator for some days.

CHARACTERISTICS

Small oxalic crystals in the pulp cause a slight burning in the mouth that is completely harmless. The fruit acid of the cactus pears causes milk products to curdle and dissolves gelatine absorptions. Therefore, the raw fruit should not be processed with these products.

TIPS ON HOW TO USE

Cactus pears are usually eaten fresh. The flavor of the cactus pear is improved when combined with sugar, liqueur, cinnamon, ginger, or honey. The fruits are also used for fruit salads, juice, and syrup. In addition, they go well with fish and meat dishes.

PREPARATION

When processing cactus pears, wear gloves, so don't get injured by the fine needles.

1. Hold the cactus pear with a fork and cut off both ends with a knife.

2. Place the fruit upright and carve strips into the skin from the top to the bottom.

3. Peel the strips of skin away from the pulp, then cut the pulp into slices or pieces.

Cape Gooseberry

ORIGIN
The cape gooseberry, also called physalis, is native to South America. At the beginning of the 19th century, it came to South Africa to the Cape of Good Hope, where it gets its name. Today, it is also cultivated in Kenya, India, Australia, and New Zealand.

DESCRIPTION AND TASTE
Its yellowish, thin, prominently ribbed calyx (parchmentlike shell) bulges like a blister around the round, orange, slightly sticky berry. The yellow flesh contains many small, soft, edible pits and tastes sweet and pleasantly acid.

PURCHASE AND STORAGE
Cape gooseberries are available usually from March to June. They can be stored only for a few days in a cool room.

TIPS ON HOW TO USE
They can be eaten fresh and are also suitable for stewed fruits, fruit salad, jam, sorbet, and marmalade. They are very popular as fillings for tarts, pies, and cakes or as decorations on desserts and beverages. The berries are easily frozen.

PREPARATION

1. Open the calyx and remove the fruit and, if you wish, cut it into slices.

2. Cape gooseberries can also be served decoratively with the shell bent back and twisted.

Cherimoya

ORIGIN
Cherimoyas (also called custard apples) belong to the Anona family and originate in the Andes Mountains of Peru and Bolivia. They are now grown commercially in California on a small scale, though the fruit is quite expensive and the quantities limited.

DESCRIPTION AND TASTE
The cherimoya is a heart-shaped fruit with a grey-to-green skin, much like that of an artichoke. It weighs from $1/2$ to $41/2$ pounds (230 g to 2 kg). The white, creamy flesh tastes mildly sweet (similar to a strawberry) and contains inedible brown seeds that can be easily removed.

PURCHASE AND STORAGE
Cherimoyas are in season during December, January, and February. A hard, unripe cherimoya ripens in a few days at room temperature. The fruit is ripe when the skin dents when slightly pressed with a finger. Cherimoyas are sold only as fresh fruits, because they cannot be preserved due to their soft consistency. Ripe cherimoyas are very fragile and must be handled delicately.

CHARACTERISTICS
Since the flesh changes color soon after it is cut, trickle lemon juice on it as soon as possible; this will also intensify the taste.

TIPS ON HOW TO USE

The cherimoya is used primarily as a table fruit, but the pulp is excellent in fruit salads in combination with mango, persimmon, and citrus fruits, and goes especially well with yogurt and other dairy products. It is also used in sauces, beverages, ice cream, and candied fruits.

PREPARATION

1. Pull out the stem. (This works especially well with ripe fruits.)

2. Cut the cherimoya into halves lengthwise and remove the seeds with the tip of the knife.

3. To eat the fruit fresh, remove the pulp with a grapefruit knife and eat with a spoon.

4. To use in recipes, scrape the pulp out with a spoon and press it through a strainer to remove the seeds.

Cherry

ORIGIN

Cherries are stone fruits that come from the Middle East. They get their name from the city Kerasos, from where the Romans once brought them home. Cherries are grown in all areas of the world where winter temperatures are not too severe. Late frosts can influence their production considerably.

DESCRIPTION AND TASTE

Cherries are divided into two groups: Sweet cherries can be either large, soft, juicy cherries or small, firm cherries. They are yellow or red and contain a strongly staining juice. Sour cherries can be dark red, sweet-sour morellos, red-brown sour cherries or light red, amarellos (glass cherries). Sour cherries have a softer pulp than do sweet ones, a very acidic flavor, and can rarely be eaten fresh.

PURCHASE AND STORAGE

Cherries are in season primarily in June and July and are difficult to transport. Undamaged fruits can be stored for about a week at 32 to 36° F (0 to 2°C).

TIPS ON HOW TO USE

Sweet cherries are usually eaten fresh, while sour cherries are often processed to make marmalade, stewed fruits, juice, fruit brandy (Kirsch), dessert, candied fruits, and ice cream, and are also used in pies and cakes. Famous cherry products are black forest cake, black forest cherry water (schnapps), Maraschino, and cherry brandy.

PREPARATION

Wash the fruits, pick off the stems, and take out the stones with a cherry stoner. Try to avoid tearing the fruits apart.

Coconut

ORIGIN

The coconut is the fruit of the coconut palm tree, which is cultivated in Sri Lanka, India, Malaysia, Indonesia, Mexico, Brazil, and the Philippines.

DESCRIPTION AND TASTE

A coconut palm tree gets from 65 to 100 feet high (20 to 30 m), grows best close to the ocean, and produces about 60 coconuts per year. It takes the fruit one year to ripen. The fruits can grow as large as a child's head and weigh about 5½ pounds (2.5 kg). The nut is surrounded by a leathery, green-brown outer skin. Underneath, there is a 1½- to 2¼-inch-thick (4 to 6 cm), dry, spongy fibrous layer. These two layers are removed in the country where the coconuts are grown. Then, the inner skin becomes visible. This layer is covered with bast fiber and has three shoot openings referred to as the "eyes." Underneath the inner skin lies the red-brown seed skin, which covers the white pulp. The coconut is hollow and contains coconut water, a light, slightly sweet liquid. As the coconut matures, the water hardens and eventually becomes pulp.

PURCHASE AND STORAGE

Coconuts are sold throughout the year. They will last for a limited time in a room with good air circulation. A coconut is ripe if the coconut water is clearly audible when the fruit is shaken. In old coconuts, the entire liquid is hardened into pulp, which tastes like soap and is inedible.

CHARACTERISTICS

The coconut contains quite a large amount of fat (36.5%). A coconut pearl forms in about one out of every 11,000 coconuts and is said to exceed the value of diamonds.

TIPS ON HOW TO USE

The pulp can be consumed fresh, as can coconut water. Grated coconut is commonly used for baking. Dried coconut meat is referred to as copra.

PREPARATION

To make coconut milk:

1. Pierce through two eyes of the coconut with a hammer and a nail and pour the coconut water into a bowl.

2. Hammer the skin of the coconut in the middle, then all around, and break the nut apart.

3. Break off the outer skin and remove the thin skin attached to the pulp with a knife or a peeler.

4. Grate the fruit pulp finely over the coconut water.

5. Pour 1 cup (¼ l) milk over the mixture, stir everything, and allow to sit for two to three hours.

6. Then pour the mixture into a cloth and press the juice through the cloth.

Cranberry

ORIGIN

The cranberry, also called the American mossberry, originated in the northern states of America and Canada. Today, it is grown primarily in Massachusetts and New Jersey. Served with turkey, cranberry sauce is part of the traditional American Thanksgiving Day meal.

DESCRIPTION AND TASTE

The ½- to ¾-inch (1.5 to 2 cm) berry can be oval, bell- or pear-shaped. The berries are dark red and taste pleasantly sour.

PURCHASE AND STORAGE

Cranberries are ripe in September or October. They are dried, cleaned, selected, and then sold in small, sealed plastic bags or in cardboard boxes. At a temperature of 34 to 38°F (1 to 3°C), the berries stay

Currant

ORIGIN
Currants originated in Europe and parts of Asia and are cultivated today in all moderate temperature zones of the earth.

DESCRIPTION AND TASTE
Currants grow on 3¼- to 6½-feet-high (1 to 2 m) shrubs, which are leafless in the winter. The berries sit like grapes on short stems and contain numerous little pits. Currants are most commonly red but come in black and white varieties as well. Red currants are smooth and taste sour and acidic. Black currants, on the other hand, taste sour and bitter. White currants—a colorless offshoot of the red currant—are less fragrant and flavorful than red ones and are rarely sold.

PURCHASE AND STORAGE
Though they are difficult to find, currants are in season from June until the end of August. They occasionally can be found in December and February from New Zealand. The berries spoil quickly and are sensitive to transport. They must be well cooled, and, even then, can be kept for only two to three days.

CHARACTERISTICS
Red currants are rich in fruit acid, pectin, and vitamin C. The black berries contain three times as much vitamin C as lemons.

TIPS ON HOW TO USE
Red currants are processed to make marmalade and jelly, and are eaten with sugar, as stewed fruits, or in Cumberland sauce. The black berries are often used to make juice, syrup, marmalade, fruit wine, brandy, and liquor (creme de Cassis).

PREPARATION
Shortly before you use them, wash the berries while they are still on the stems, let them drain, and then pick them off the stems. They must be processed quickly, so that they do not lose much juice.

fresh for up to three months. There is the danger, though, that a portion of the berries will shrink or rot.

CHARACTERISTICS
The berries are rich in vitamin C and were, in former times, taken by seamen on trips as a remedy for scurvy.

TIPS ON HOW TO USE
Even though it is possible to eat the berry raw, it is unusual. Cranberries are usually processed to make sauces, jams, jellies, ice cream, cakes, and syrup. It is especially common to serve it with game or poultry.

PREPARATION
The berries should be carefully selected and washed under running water.

Date

ORIGIN:

The date palm originates in the subtropical areas of Africa and can reach 100 years. Most of the world's cultivation is in Iraq, Iran, Egypt, Israel, Saudi Arabia, Algeria, Pakistan, and Morocco.

DESCRIPTION AND TASTE

The red-brown, oval dates are $1\frac{1}{4}$ to 2 inches long (3 to 5 cm). They contain a yellowish white pulp and a hard, brown pit. The pulp tastes sweet, like honey.

PURCHASE AND STORAGE

Dates are sold dried and in small boxes. They are dried in the country where they are grown, either in the sun, or in special ovens. Stored in a cool and dry place, they will last almost indefinitely. Fresh dates are frozen immediately after they are harvested and then defrosted before they are sold. Because they have a low fluid content and a high sugar content, the fruits survive this treatment very well.

TIPS ON HOW TO USE

Dates can be eaten either fresh or dried. They are used in sauces, fruit salads, appetizers, and entrees. They are served as a dessert, filled with marzipan, or as a confectionery, dipped in chocolate.

PREPARATION

1. Slightly cut into the skin of the date with the tip of a knife and pull it in strips from the fruit.

2. Cut the date open lengthwise with the knife up to the pit, separate the fruit halves, and remove the pit.

Fig

ORIGIN

The small fig tree most likely originated in the Orient, where it is very widespread. Today, it is also grown in Turkey, Greece, Italy, Spain, Portugal, Southern France, and Brazil. Nearly all of the figs grown commercially in the United States are grown in California.

DESCRIPTION AND TASTE

There are both male and female fig trees, the female trees being the only ones that bear fruit. The female fig tree produces fruit for the first time when it is eight years old, but then for about 40 years. Most fig trees bloom three times a year, and figs are classified as early harvest, main harvest, or late harvest. The fruit is about 3 inches long (8 cm) and has the shape of a pear. The skin is yellow-green, solid green, red, or brown-violet. The lighter fruits are more sour than the darker ones.

PURCHASE AND STORAGE

Fresh figs from California are in season from June to November. Dried figs come mainly from Turkey, Greece, and California. Fresh figs easily go bad (they get moldy), are very sensitive to pressure, and are therefore sold individually wrapped in paper. Dried figs last for several months. The white layer on the fruits is secreted sugar, not mold.

TIPS ON HOW TO USE

Fresh figs should be eaten well cooled and peeled; dried figs are eaten with the skin on. Figs are also used for cooking and baking as well as in appetizers, meat and fish dishes, desserts, cakes, marmalade, jam, syrup, and spirits.

PREPARATION

2. Peel off the skin in strips from the fruit.

1. If the fig is fresh and hard, cut off the stem and the bottom thinly.

3. If the fig is soft, cut the fruit into four pieces, then peel the skin off the fruit starting on the pointed side.

Grape

ORIGIN

Grapes are said to have originated in Transcaucasia and Central Asia. Today, they are grown worldwide and are among the most common fruits. Only about 10% of the grape production is used for table grapes—the remainder is pressed and dried. The main areas where grapes are grown are Italy, Spain, France, West Germany, the Balkan Peninsula, Australia, and the United States.

DESCRIPTION AND TASTE

Grapes hang, arranged in clusters, from climbing shrubs. The berries are oval, green or red, and can have either thick or thin skins. The larger grapes contain more tannic acid in the skin than the smaller varieties. There are many varieties of grapes. Unfortunately, a description of these varieties would go beyond the scope of this book, therefore we have decided to forego it. The berries of some varieties of grapes are covered with a thin, flourlike rime, which can be wiped off. It is created because of the change of the humidity of air between day and night. When this rime is reduced, a waxlike natural film is created. Grapes usually contain up to five pits, though there are pitless varieties.

PURCHASE AND STORAGE

Grapes are sold throughout the year. They have to be harvested when they are ripe, since they do not ripen once they are picked.

TIPS ON HOW TO USE

Grapes are eaten fresh or pressed to make wine or juice, dried to make raisins, or used as garnish for cheese and cold cut platters. They are also commonly used in pies, fruit salads, sauces, and desserts.

PREPARATION

1. Wash the grapes under lukewarm water to remove dust and any residual insecticides. Then pick the berries off the stems.

2. Cut the berries in half and remove the pits with the tip of the knife.

The grapefruit is usually eaten fresh or in fruit salads. The bitter taste can be moderated with sugar or honey. Its juice is often combined with spirits or liqueurs. In addition to making juice, the fruits are processed to make jam, marmalade, candied fruits, sorbet, and sweets.

PREPARATION

1. To eat the fruit fresh, cut in half crosswise, remove the pits, and separate the fruit segments with a knife.

2. Separate the pulp from the skin with a grapefruit knife. Now the pulp can be eaten with a teaspoon.

Grapefruit

ORIGIN
The grapefruit originated in the West Indies (Puerto Rico). It is a descendant of the pomelo, a larger fruit. Most grapefruit is grown in the United States, with 60% of the world production concentrated primarily in Florida, Texas, Arizona, and California.

DESCRIPTION AND TASTE
The grapefruit is larger than the orange, but smaller than the pomelo. The fruit is firm and has a smooth, light yellow-to-reddish-yellow skin. The yellow-to-red pulp is juicy and has a sharp, sour, and somewhat bitter taste. It sometimes contains pits.

PURCHASE AND STORAGE
Grapefruit is sold throughout the year. When stored at temperatures of 46 to 59°F (8 to 15°C), the fruits last for several months.

CHARACTERISTICS
The juice and pulp contain bitter substances, which accumulate especially in the white skin underneath the peel. The fruit is rich in vitamin C. The pulp stimulates the appetite and furthers digestion. If grapefruit or grapefruit juice is processed with products that contain protein (e.g., gelatine or milk products), the protein is decomposed (the food turns bitter) after sitting for a while, and the bonding or absorption of the gelatine is canceled.

3. If individual segments are needed, cut off the peel from the top and bottom of the whole fruit, so that no white peel remains on the pulp.

4. Then cut the individual segments out of the fruit walls above a container.

5. Squeeze the juice by hand out of the fruit walls.

Guava

ORIGIN

The guava is the fruit of the evergreen guava tree. It probably originated in either Brazil or Mexico, and today it is found in most tropical countries. The areas where it is grown are India, South Africa, Mexico, Columbia, Brazil, Florida, California, and Hawaii.

DESCRIPTION AND TASTE

The guava tree is 9 to 20 feet high (3 to 6 m) and is also cultivated as a shrub. The apple-shaped fruit has a greenish yellow, waxy skin. The yellow-to-pink pulp is divided into four or five chambers and contains numerous pits. The pulp tastes sweetish-sour. The strawberry guava and the wild guava are relatives of the guava.

PURCHASE AND STORAGE

Guavas are imported throughout the year. In the country where they are grown, they are harvested for export before they are fully ripe and then carefully individually packed. They have to be sold quickly and can be stored only for a couple of days. In order to fully ripen in a short time, a temperature of 44 to 50°F (7 to 10°C) is necessary. Guavas are also available in cans.

TIPS ON HOW TO USE

When sprinkled with sugar and lemon juice, the guava tastes good in fruit salads. In addition, it can be excellent when combined with heavy cream or yogurt.

PREPARATION

1. Peel the guava thinly with a knife.

2. Cut the fruit into slices or pieces.

Kiwi

ORIGIN

The kiwi, also called the Chinese gooseberry, comes from China and Taiwan. Today, it is grown predominately in New Zealand, but is also cultivated in Australia, California, South Africa, Chile, Japan, and some Mediterranean countries.

DESCRIPTION AND TASTE

Kiwis are the fruits of a climbing, shrublike plant. The fruits hang like grapes from the tendrils, which are usually tied to poles. The oval fruit is about the size of an egg and weighs 2 to 3½ ounces (60 to 100 g). The skin is, at first, dark green, then later becomes brown and hairy. The green, slightly glassy pulp contains many edible black pits. Its taste is very refreshing, similar to melon and strawberry.

PURCHASE AND STORAGE

Kiwis are sold throughout the year. Ripe fruits dent when slightly pressed with a finger. The fruit ripens especially quickly at room temperature when stored with apples.

CHARACTERISTICS

Fresh kiwis contain an enzyme which splits protein, causes milk products to curdle and become bitter, and dissolves the absorption of gelatine. If the fruit has been blanched briefly, however, it can be used with milk products and gelatine, because the enzyme is inactive at 104°F (40°C).

TIPS ON HOW TO USE

Kiwis are commonly eaten fresh, either alone or in fruit salads. In addition, the fruit is used for baking and cooking and is also suitable for making juice, lemonade, liquor, jelly, and stewed fruits.

PREPARATION

1. You can eat kiwis fresh by cutting the fruit in half and spooning the pulp out of the skin. You can also peel kiwi thinly with a peeler. Riper, somewhat soft fruits can be peeled with a fruit knife.

2. Cut out the stem in a wedge and divide the fruit into slices, cubes, or pieces.

Lemon

ORIGIN

The lemon is native to West Asia, Southern China, and India. Today, it can be found in subtropical areas all over the world. Lemons can not tolerate extremes, either of cold or heat. The main areas where lemons are grown are Italy, Spain, Greece, California, Florida, and Central and South America.

DESCRIPTION AND TASTE

The fruits grow on evergreen lemon trees, which can grow up to 23 feet high (7 m). The oval or egg-shaped fruit weighs 1¾ to 3¾ ounces (50 to 120 g). The outside of the skin is either rough or smooth, green or yellow (or somewhere in between). The inside of the skin is white, spongy, and quite dry. The pulp consists of seven to ten segments filled with pits, is very juicy, and extremely sour.

PURCHASE AND STORAGE

Lemons are available throughout the year, since they are grown worldwide. Usually they are harvested before they are fully ripe. They ripen when stored at about 50°F (10°C). The fruit is ripe when the skin begins to shine.

CHARACTERISTICS

Lemons contain about five percent citric acid and a lot of vitamin C. The skin contains essential oils, which are used in the baking and cosmetics industries. If the skin of the lemon is to be used, use only organically grown fruits.

TIPS ON HOW TO USE

Lemon juice and lemon peel are used as a spice for the seasoning of dishes, desserts, soups, and sauces as well as fish, meat, and poultry dishes. The candied skin is used in baking. In addition, the lemon is used in the production of ice cream, lemonade, and other beverages.

PREPARATION

1. To use the skin, wash the organic lemon, dry it, and either grate the skin with a zester or tear it off in strips.

2. Halve the fruit and squeeze it to get lemon juice.

3. Lemon segments are prepared in the same manner as orange segments (see page 31).

Lime

ORIGIN

Limes, also called citrons, are citrus fruits. They come from Southeast Asia and are cultivated today in many tropical countries, as well as in Egypt, Mexico, Brazil, and Florida.

DESCRIPTION AND TASTE

Limes grow on thorned evergreen shrubs or on 13- to 17-feet-high (4 to 5 m) trees. The fruits are egg-shaped and have a thin, shiny skin, which is dark green at the beginning and eventually turns greenish yellow. The pulp tastes strongly sour and contains about twice as much juice as a lemon. The fruits are mostly without pits.

PURCHASE AND STORAGE

Limes are available throughout the year. Some limes are harvested when they are green and can be easily stored; others are harvested when they are yellow-green and must be sold quickly. Limes are usually organically grown. It is much harder to store limes than lemons—the skin shrivels quickly, and the fruit loses juice rapidly. Limes can be stored in the refrigerator for six to eight weeks.

TIPS ON HOW TO USE

Limes are used in ice cream, sorbets, cold soups, and desserts. The skin is used as a baking ingredient, and lime juice is the basis for many fruit juice beverages. They are prepared just like the lemon.

Loquat

ORIGIN
The loquat originated in China. It is also called Japanese meddler, Brazilian apricot, or, in Italy, nespoli. Loquats are also cultivated in Northern India, Thailand, in some Mediterranean countries, California, and Florida, as well as in South and Central America.

DESCRIPTION AND TASTE
Loquats are the false fruits of a 17- to 33-feet-high (5 to 10 m) evergreen tree. The small, egg-shaped fruits are 1¼ to 3 inches long (3 to 8 cm). The light yellow-to-dark orange skin is tough and covered with hair. The pulp is very juicy and tastes pleasantly sweetish-sour. The fruit contains three to five shiny bean-shaped pits, which are used like almonds.

PURCHASE AND STORAGE
Loquats have the earliest harvest time of any spring fruit: they are in season from March through May in Florida and until June in California. Since the fruits have a sensitive skin, they have to be transported carefully and must be sold as quickly as possible. The fruits can be stored at 39 to 43°F (4 to 6°C) for one to two weeks. Loquats are also sold in cans.

TIPS ON HOW TO USE
Poaching loquats in sugar syrup brings out the natural flavor. Very ripe fruits lose their strong acid and can then be eaten fresh or, like plums, apricots, or cherries, can be processed to make such products as stewed fruits, ice cream, sorbets, or fruit salad. Loquats are suitable as a side dish with poultry, meat, and fish dishes.

PREPARATION
1. Peel the loquats with a knife or pull off the skin.
2. Halve the fruits and remove the pits.

Lychee

ORIGIN
The lychee is a native of southern China. The word lychee (or litchi) is derived from the Chinese "Lee Chee," and means "giver of the pleasure of life." Besides in China, lychees are cultivated in India, Australia, New Zealand, Madagascar, Hawaii, South Africa, Kenya, Brazil, and Florida.

DESCRIPTION AND TASTE
Lychees are the fruits of a 33- to 40-feet-high (10 to 12 m) tree, which can produce up to 660 pounds (300 kg) of fruit per year. The fruit grows hanging together in panicles, is 1 to 1½ inches (2.5 to 4 cm) in diameter, and resembles pinecones. The leathery, scaly skin is cherry red and turns brown when in storage. Underneath is the jelly-like, sweetish-sour pulp, which shines through the skin and smells like roses. The pulp contains an inedible brown pit.

PURCHASE AND STORAGE
Lychees are sold throughout the year. The fruits have to be harvested when they are ripe, because they will not ripen later. At room temperature, they can be stored for about one week.

CHARACTERISTICS

Lychees contain a large quantity of sugar and vitamin C. When they are cooked, the aroma is easily lost; therefore, the fruits should be heated up only briefly.

TIPS ON HOW TO USE

Lychees are usually eaten fresh, but they are also well suited for fruit salads, cocktails, stewed fruits, sorbets, and jellies. They are also available dried or in cans, though the taste is not as intense.

PREPARATION

1. Break the skin open with your fingers and remove it.

2. Cut into the pulp with a small knife and remove the pit.

Mango

ORIGIN

Besides the banana and the pineapple, the mango is the most important tropical fruit. It comes from India, where many of the original mango forests can still be found. There, it is considered a national fruit and given religious significance. Today, mangos are also grown in virtually all tropical regions of the world, mainly Latin America, South Africa, Haiti, Mexico, Israel, Egypt, and Florida.

DESCRIPTION AND TASTE

The fruits of the 33- to 100-feet-high (10 to 30 m) mango tree are stone fruits. They hang on long stems and vary in size, shape, and color; mangos can be as small as apricots, as large as melons, either round or oval, and egg- or kidney-shaped. The leathery skin is green, yellow, orange, or red. These differences occur even among fruits on the same tree. An average mango weighs approximately 10 ounces (300 g), though it can also weigh up to 4½ pounds (2 kg). The yellow or red, juicy, sweet pulp surrounds the relatively large, longish stone, which is often difficult to remove.

PURCHASE AND STORAGE

Mangos can be purchased throughout the year. The fruits are sensitive to transport and are therefore harvested unripe. They then ripen in storage places at temperatures between 77 and 86°F (25 and 30°C)—relatively high temperatures. Cold temperatures lead to brown spots and rotting. A mango is ripe when it dents when slightly pressed with a finger and when it gives off an aromatic scent. Mangos that are bought unripe ripen at home within one week at temperatures over 59°F (15°C).

CHARACTERISTICS

Mangos are very juicy. But careful, because the juice leaves brown stains on clothing, which are difficult to remove.

TIPS ON HOW TO USE

Mangos are often eaten fresh, though the ripe fruit can also be used to make salads, desserts, ice cream, sorbets, stewed fruits, juice, soups, sauces, jellies, and jams. Green, unripe fruits are processed to make sharp pastes, chutneys, and pickles. A recipe for mango chutney appears on page 74.

PREPARATION

1. Peel firm, green mangos with a peeler.

2. To remove the stone, place the mango upright and cut off the pulp with the knife along the stone.

3. Scrape the pulp off the stone with the help of a fork and with the back of the knife.

4. If the fruits are ripe and soft, cut off the pulp and spoon it out of the skin.

5. Cut the pulp into pieces, slices, or small cubes.

Mangosteen

ORIGIN

The mangosteen comes from Malaysia, but it is also grown in Southeast Asia, Central America, and Brazil. In Asia, the fruit is quite expensive and considered a delicacy.

DESCRIPTION AND TASTE

The mangosteen grows on a 40- to 50-feet-high (12 to 15 m) evergreen tree. The fruits weigh about 2½ ounces (80 g) and are round and slightly flattened at the top and the bottom. The skin is reddish brown-to-dark violet (often speckled red) and contains a resinous juice which contains tannic acid. The pearly white pulp is divided into four or more segments and contains longish, yellow-green, edible pits. The pulp tastes tangy, sweet, and somewhat spicy.

PURCHASE AND STORAGE

The fruit has to be harvested when it is ripe, since it does not ripen later on. If it is not cooled, it goes bad quickly. For that reason, mangosteens are relatively expensive and rarely sold in the United States.

CHARACTERISTICS

The skin contains tannin. It dries, when stored for a long time, and is then hard to open. The purple juice of the skin causes stains that are difficult to remove.

TIPS ON HOW TO USE

The mangosteen is commonly eaten fresh, well cooled, and with the pits. Especially in combination with heavy cream and ice cream, it is popular as a dessert. Mangosteens also go well with fish and meat dishes, but should only be heated up, not completely cooked; otherwise they lose their taste.

PREPARATION

1. Cut the firm skin open with a knife.

2. Take out the pulp and, as with tangerines, divide into individual segments.

Melon

ORIGIN

The melon is a native of the Middle East. The word melon is derived from the Greek word that means big apple. Melons are grown in warm countries worldwide, especially in the Mediterranean countries, Israel, Hungary, Bulgaria, Morocco, Turkey, and the United States.

DESCRIPTION AND TASTE

Melons weigh, depending on the variety, up to 8¾ pounds (4 kg). Their numerous seeds can be easily removed with a spoon. The following is a list of some common melons:

Cantaloupe: Named after the place where it was grown, Cantalupo near Rome, the cantaloupe weighs approximately 1 pound (454 g) and is the smallest melon. It is round with white, yellow, or green smooth or ribbed skin. The yellow-orange, very aromatic pulp tastes sweet and spicy. Other versions of the cantaloupe are the Charentais (France) and the Ogen (Israel).

Casaba: This large, round melon, with a green-to-yellow skin and a pale green pulp, is pointed at the stem end. Other types of Casabas are Canary, a brilliant yellow variety, and Santa Claus, a smaller melon with dark green and yellow skin.

Crenshaw: This melon is a cross between a Casaba and a Cantaloupe. Its green skin becomes yellow as it ripens, and its pulp is sweet, juicy, very fragrant, and salmon colored.

Honeydew: This oval fruit has a cream-colored, green, or light brown, netted skin. It has yellow or green pulp that is extremely sweet, particularly when vine ripened. Look for cream-colored honeydews with a strong aroma at the blossom end. Watermelons will be discussed in a separate chapter (see page 45). Other melon varieties are Persian, Sharlyn, and Juan Canary.

PURCHASE AND STORAGE

Melons are sold throughout the year. A ripe melon dents when slightly pressed with the finger and has an intense smell at the base of the fruit. Unripe melons ripen at room temperature in a few days and should not be stored in the refrigerator.

CHARACTERISTICS

Melons are a healthy, low-calorie food. They are composed of water and sugar, and are also high in vitamins C and A.

TIPS ON HOW TO USE

Melons are eaten fresh, served in fruit salad, marinated with spirits or liqueurs, pureed to make cold soups or sorbets, or as appetizers. Melons go well with both sweet or salty foods.

PREPARATION

1. Halve the melon lengthwise and remove the seeds with a spoon.

2. To serve fresh, cut the fruit halves into pieces and loosen the pulp from the skin with a knife.

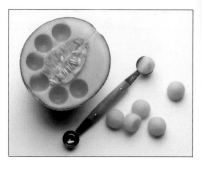

3. For melon balls, scoop out balls with a melon baller from the halves. Remove the seeds only when the first round has been scooped out.

4. For decoration, cut into the fruit in zigzags from the middle all around, pull the halves apart, and remove the seeds.

Nectarine

ORIGIN
The nectarine descends from the peach, which originated in China. The main regions where nectarines are grown are France, Italy, Spain, Greece, Israel, and California.

DESCRIPTION AND TASTE
Nectarines are a variety of the peach; it is not uncommon for peach trees to produce nectarines, or for nectarine trees to produce peaches. Nectarines are stone fruits and distinguish themselves from the peach by their smooth skin and their firm pulp.

PURCHASE AND STORAGE
Nectarines are available through-out the year. From May to December, they are harvested in the United States, the peak of the domestic market being July through August. From January

through April, they are imported from South America. They are very difficult to transport, though, and must be harvested before they are fully ripe. When they ripen later, they lose some of their taste.

Nashi

ORIGIN
The nashi, also called Chinese, Japanese, or Asian pear, comes from Northern China, Korea, and Japan. Today, they are also culti-vated in Taiwan, New Zealand, Australia, Chile, and California.

DESCRIPTION AND TASTE
The nashi grows on shrubs, which are supported by a pergola system. There are more than 25 varieties. The Chinese type resembles our Bartlett pear, though it is some-what larger and has a softer pulp with many seeds. The Japanese type is shaped like the Golden Delicious apple and has a firm, seedless pulp. The variety that is most commonly enjoyed in the United States is the Twentieth Century, a smooth, round, green-to-yellow fruit with sweet, mild, and juicy flesh.

PURCHASE AND STORAGE
Nashis are available throughout the year. They can be stored at 36 to 40°F. (2 to 4°C.) for some weeks.

TIPS ON HOW TO USE
Nashis are usually eaten fresh, but can also be used in fruit salads, stewed fruits, marmalades, and desserts.

PREPARATION
Nashis are peeled like apples or pears, halved, and the seeds removed (see page 7).

CHARACTERISTICS

In contrast to the peach, most nectarine varieties are freestones—that is, they have a stone that is easily removed. Nectarines are a good source of vitamin C.

TIPS ON HOW TO USE

Nectarines are often consumed as table fruit. Though there is a subtle difference in flavor, they can be processed like peaches in most dishes. Because of their firm pulp, they can be easily divided into decorative pieces.

PREPARATION

The preparation is the same as that of the peach (see page 34).

Orange

ORIGIN

The orange comes from Southern China. Today it is grown primarily in Israel, Brazil, the Mediterranean, Mexico, India, South Africa, Australia, Florida, and California.

DESCRIPTION AND TASTE

Oranges are the fruits of the 10- to 26-feet-high (3 to 8 m) orange tree. They come in various sizes, shapes (round or oval), colors (yellow, orange, or red), and tastes. Between the skin and the flesh of the orange, there is a thick, white skin, which is not eaten. The pulp is divided into 8 to 12 segments, contains pits, and tastes anywhere from very sweet to quite sour. The following is a list of the most common varieties.

Sweet oranges have a light pulp and are sold by brand names such as Naveline, Navel, Navel Late, Valencia (Spain), Jaffa (Israel), Outspan (South Africa), and Sunkist (California). These are the most widely eaten oranges.

Halfblood oranges have a slightly red pulp and are commonly sold as Washington Sanguina, Bloodoval (both from Spain), Moro (Morocco), and Tarocco (Sicily).

Blood oranges have a blood red pulp and are sometimes called Sanguinello. They are usually imported from the Mediterranean but are now being grown in California.

Bitter or sour oranges (Seville oranges) are not eaten fresh. Their skin, which is easily removed, is used as a spice for meat and fish dishes and as a baking ingredient.

The pulp can also be processed to make marmalade, jam, liquor (curacao), and bitter beverages. **Kumquats** (dwarf oranges) are not actually oranges (or even citrus fruits), though the two are often grouped together. They are very small, oval fruits $\frac{3}{4}$ to $1\frac{1}{4}$ inches in diameter (2 to 3 cm). Because their rind is very sweet (in contrast to their very tart pulp), they can be eaten with the rind on. Be sure you wash them well beforehand. **Limequats** are a cross between an orange and a lime.

PURCHASE AND STORAGE

Harvested oranges do not ripen any further. Therefore, only fruits with a controlled sugar-acid content are sold. The skin color is not a reliable indication of ripeness, because in order to develop their orange-yellow color, the fruits need night temperatures of around 32°F (0°C). Therefore, fruits with a slightly green skin can be fully ripe. In order to protect the fruits from rotting during transport and storage, they are washed immediately after the harvest and are often covered with wax. At a temperature of 36 to 41°F (2 to 5°C), they will last for several weeks.

TIPS ON HOW TO USE

Oranges are usually eaten fresh or squeezed. If the skin is to be used as a spice (orange zest), use only organically grown oranges. Even then, you should wash them thoroughly beforehand.

PREPARATION

1. To use the skin of the orange, wash the organic orange, dry it, and grate the skin with a fine grater.

2. To get orange zest, wash the organic orange, dry it and tear off the skin in strips by hand or with an orange zester.

3. To get segments, cut off the peel on the top and bottom. Then cut off the skin with a knife from top to bottom so that the white skin is removed as well.

4. Cut the segments out of the fruit walls.

5. Squeeze the juice out of the walls of the fruit by hand.

6. In order to remove the pits from a kumquat, cut the fruit crosswise and press out the pits with a slight pressure onto the skin or with a sharp knife.

Papaya

ORIGIN

The papaya comes from Central America. The chief areas where it is grown are Central and South America, Florida, Hawaii, India, and Africa.

DESCRIPTION AND TASTE

Papayas are the fruits of an approximately 33½-feet-high (10 m) tree, and they come in more than 70 varieties. The fruits are club-shaped and have a leathery, green-to-golden yellow skin. The light yellow-to-orange pulp is soft and tastes mildly sweet, much like a melon. The inside of the fruit is hollow and contains many small pits. An average papaya weighs approximately 1 pound (454 g).

PURCHASE AND STORAGE

Papaya is available throughout the year. They should not be harvested too early, because they do not ripen later on. You can tell a papaya is ripe when brown spots develop on the skin, and if the skin dents when slightly pressed with a finger. Papayas are difficult to transport and can be kept in the refrigerator for only a few days.

CHARACTERISTICS

Papayas contain the enzyme papain, which splits protein. Therefore, fresh papayas must not be processed with milk products or gelatine. Through brief cooking, though, the enzyme will be inactivated.

TIPS ON HOW TO USE

Ripe papayas are eaten fresh, with lemon or lime juice sprinkled on them. Unripe fruits (which still have green skin) taste acidic and sour and are used (like pumpkins) as vegetables. Ripe papayas can also be used for fruit salad, ice cream, marmalade, jelly, and desserts.

PREPARATION

2. Halve the fruit and scrape out the pits with a spoon.

1. Peel the papaya thinly with a potato peeler.

3. Cut the pulp into pieces or slices.

Passion Fruit

ORIGIN

Passion fruit, or Purple Granadilla, originated in Central and South America but has spread quickly to regions with similar climates, such as Australia, New Zealand, Kenya, Senegal, the Ivory Coast, Sri Lanka, Madagascar, California, and Hawaii.

DESCRIPTION AND TASTE

There are several hundred varieties of passion fruit. Many of the varieties produce enchantingly beautiful blossoms. Some fruits resemble little lemons, others large, crumpled plums. The skin is yellow-to-orange, green-to-purple, or dark red-to-violet. All passion fruit contains a green-grey, white, or yellow jellylike pulp, and contains many small pits. The pulp of the passion fruit tastes pleasantly tart and sweet. Passion fruit can be divided into two major groups. The first (and most common) type weighs about 1¼ ounces (38 g) and has a smooth, leathery, purple skin. It starts to shrink some days after the harvest—a sign of ripeness. The second type, the yellow passion fruit, is a long, lemon yellow or sometimes light green fruit that weighs usually around 3 ounces (90 g) and has a thicker skin than the purple variety.

PURCHASE AND STORAGE

Passion fruits are sold mainly in the summer months. At temperatures of 41 to 50°F (5 to 10°C), they can be stored for up to two weeks.

CHARACTERISTICS

Raw passion fruits will not allow dishes with gelatine to become firm. Used with milk products, they can cause the food to become bitter, since they have an enzyme that splits protein.

TIPS ON HOW TO USE

Fresh passion fruits are halved and eaten with a spoon (without removing the pits). In order to make juice, the pulp is pushed (again, with the pits) through a strainer. Passion fruit can also be used in fruit salads, ice cream, sorbets, jellies, desserts, cakes and pies, and mixed drinks.

PREPARATION

Halve the fruit with a knife, scrape the pulp out with a spoon, and push it through a strainer.

Peach

ORIGIN

The peach comes from China, and is cultivated today in almost all warm, moderate areas, including Italy, France, Spain, Greece, South America, Australia, South Africa, and the United States. In the United States, most peaches are grown in California and in the South.

DESCRIPTION AND TASTE

Peaches are stone fruits. They grow on low trees in orchards specifically created for their cultivation. The fruits are round, sometimes with pointed ends, with a longitudinal groove, and a deepened stem. The skin is green, yellow, or red, and covered with many fine hairs—peach fuzz. The white, yellow, or (in blood peaches) red flesh tastes juicy and sweet and is highly aromatic. A hard, oval, grooved stone is contained within the pulp. The white early peach varieties have a stone which is easier to remove than the yellow later varieties.

PURCHASE AND STORAGE

Peaches are sold throughout the year, though the peak of the season in the United States is June through August. They are even more sensitive to pressure than nectarines and are also picked when they are unripe. When they ripen in storage halls, they lose some of their taste. In special cool houses they can be stored up to four weeks. Unfortunately, at home they can be stored only for a short time. When purchasing peaches, look for unbruised, firm, and colorful fruit.

TIPS ON HOW TO USE

Peaches are eaten fresh or used in fruit salads, marmalade, ice cream, sorbet, cold soup, juices, wine, brandy, and liqueur. They are also wonderful in cakes and pies. Peaches are also sold in cans. The stones, which contain oil, are processed to make liqueur (Persico).

PREPARATION

1. To remove the skin, slightly cut into the peach crosswise, dip it briefly in hot water, then in cold water. Then peel the skin off with a knife.

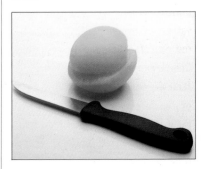

2. To halve the fruit, cut along the longitudinal groove up to the stone, turn the two halves in opposite directions, and separate them.

3. Either remove the stone by hand, or, if necessary, cut it out.

Pear

ORIGIN
The pear was eaten as early as the Bronze Age. It originated in Turkey and Afghanistan but today is grown worldwide. The areas where it is grown are France, Belgium, Italy, Holland, Austria, Germany, Chile, Argentina, South Africa, China, and the United States.

DESCRIPTION AND TASTE
The taste ranges from slightly sour to honey-sweet. The color of the skin varies from yellow-brown to green or red. Some common varieties are Clapp Favorite, Louise Bonne de Jersey, Bartlett, and d'Anjou.

PURCHASE AND STORAGE
Unlike apples, pears can be stored only for a limited amount of time. Fresh pears, though, are sold throughout the year. Unripe pears ripen quickly at room temperature.

CHARACTERISTICS
Peeled pears turn brown quickly at the surface and should be processed quickly or sprinkled with lemon juice.

TIPS ON HOW TO USE
Pears are often eaten fresh but are also used in preserves or stewed fruits, marmalade, juice, liqueur, or pear schnapps.

PREPARATION
Pears are prepared like apples (see page 7).

Persimmon

ORIGIN
The persimmon, also called kaki, date plum, kaki plum, or Japanese apricot, has its origins in China and Japan. While it is still widely popular in the Orient, it is also grown in Southern Europe, India, Australia, Brazil, Israel, California, and Florida.

DESCRIPTION AND TASTE
These orange, tomatolike fruits have four large sepals at the rudiment. The skin is thin, smooth, and shiny, and the fruit weighs between $3\frac{1}{3}$ and 13 ounces (100 and 400 g) and has a diameter of up to 3 inches (8 cm). The jellylike pulp is filled with pits. Ripe persimmons are sweet, but unripe fruits have an extremely unpleasant flavor. The Sharon fruit, a variety from Israel, has no pits, a softer skin, and contains less tannic acids.

PURCHASE AND STORAGE
Persimmons are packed individually in flat boxes, because they are very sensitive to pressure. You can find persimmons on the market from late fall through winter, although sometimes they are available at other times (usually from Chile). Persimmons are picked while still unripe for export, and they ripen in transport and in the storage rooms. A ripe persimmon has a shiny pulp that glimmers through the skin. Once ripe, it should be eaten as quickly as possible. Persimmons can be stored unripe at a temperature of 32 to 38°F (0 to 3°C) for up to two weeks.

CHARACTERISTICS
Persimmons are considered a good source of energy, because they are rich in carbohydrates, which are quickly utilized by the body. Persimmons are harvested only when they are fully ripe.

TIPS ON HOW TO USE

Persimmons are usually eaten fresh. But they also taste wonderful in combination with vanilla ice cream, heavy cream, cottage cheese, or yogurt. In addition, they are processed to make stewed fruit, jam, ice cream, sorbet, juice, and syrup.

PREPARATION

1. Cut out the stem and peel off the skin in strips with a small knife.

2. Cut the fruit into slices or cubes.

Pineapple

ORIGIN

The pineapple, the most common tropical fruit, originated in the low-lands of Brazil. Today, the main areas where it is grown are the West Indies, Cuba, Columbia, Brazil, Hawaii, South Africa, and the Ivory Coast. If the fruits are to be exported, they are harvested, like bananas, while they are unripe.

DESCRIPTION AND TASTE

The color of the skin, which can vary from dark green to yellow to dark orange, does not reveal anything about the degree of ripeness. Thus, a green pineapple can most certainly be ripe. This very aromatic and juicy fruit weighs between $2\frac{1}{3}$ and $8\frac{3}{4}$ pounds (1 and 4 kg). The baby pineapple gets to be only about 1 pound (454 g).

PURCHASE AND STORAGE

There are three ways to determine if a pineapple is ripe: it gives off an intense scent at the stem; the skin dents when slightly pressed with the finger; and the leaves can be easily pulled out. Ripe pineapples should be stored at about 46°F (8°C), but when stored in the refrigerator, the aroma suffers and the fruit develops slightly brown spots.

CHARACTERISTICS

The fruit of the pineapple is rich in vitamins and minerals. Fresh pineapple contains an enzyme that causes egg whites to split, does not permit gelatine to get completely stiff, and causes milk products to turn bitter. The enzyme is inactive from a temperature of 104°F (40°C) or above. Therefore, cooked pineapple can be processed with gelatine and milk products without any problems.

TIPS ON HOW TO USE
Pineapple is especially suitable for fruit salads and desserts, but it goes just as well with poultry and meat dishes, and on tarts, and pizzas.

PREPARATION

1. Break or cut off the blossom and leaves, then cut off a lid at the top and slice off the bottom until the fruit becomes visible.

2. Keep the fruit upright and cut off the skin as thinly as possible in strips from the top to the bottom. If possible, remove the "eyes" of the fruit while doing this.

3. If you have not already done so, cut out the "eyes" with a small, pointed knife.

4. For slices, slice the fruit and remove the woody stalk with the help of an apple corer.

5. For pieces, cut the unpeeled fruit lengthwise, then cut the stalk off with a knife. Remove the pulp of the fruit from the skin with a small knife and cut it into pieces. The pineapple pieces can be placed in the skin, with the skin serving as a container.

Plum

ORIGIN
Plums are the fruits of the plum tree, which originated in Asia, Europe, and North America. Today, they are grown primarily in Italy, Spain, the former Yugoslavia, Bulgaria, and the United States.

DESCRIPTION AND TASTE
Though there are many varieties of plums, they are generally divided into two major groups:
European plums are egg-shaped fruits with blue or purple, rimy skin. The rime protects the plum from drying out and needs only to be wiped off. The yellow, firm pulp of the European plum tastes juicy and sweet and contains a flat stone, which can be easily removed. European plums are the only plum variety that is dried. A variety of this group is the Damson, a plum named for its place of origin, Damascus. The Damson is very tart and is especially suitable for pre-

serves and jams. Other European varieties are the President and the Empress.

Japanese plums have a yellow to red (but never purple) skin and a yellow-to-dark red, very sweet pulp. The stone is very hard to remove. Japanese plums are generally eaten fresh. Some common varieties are LaRoda, Eldorado, Queen Anne, Santa Rosa, and Queen Rosa.

PURCHASE AND STORAGE

Plums are available May through September, though they are at their peak in June, July, and August. When purchasing plums, look for firm, colorful, unbruised fruits. Unripe fruits will ripen at room temperature.

TIPS ON TO USE

Plums are eaten fresh or processed to make jam, stewed fruits, marmalade, cake fillings, sorbet, wine, juice, or brandy.

PREPARATION

1. When preparing small fruits, remove the stone with a knife.

2. Large fruits should be cut open along the seam, the halves pulled apart, and the stone removed.

Pomegranate

ORIGIN

The pomegranate tree has its origin in West Asia, though today it is grown in the entire Mediterranean area. Its picture is even in the Spanish coat of arms. The city and province of Granada were named after it. The bright red blossom has always been considered a symbol of love and its fruit a symbol of fertility. All pomegranates that are produced in the United States are grown in California.

DESCRIPTION AND TASTE

The pomegranate is a false fruit and weighs about 1 pound (454 g). It has yellow, orange, or red leathery skin. The inside of the fruit is rich in juice and is divided into chambers by white skins. These chambers contain seeds, which are each surrounded by light-to-dark red, jellylike skins. These skins are the edible part of the fruit. Their taste is uniquely sweet-tart.

PURCHASE AND STORAGE

Pomegranates are usually available in fall and early winter but are at their peak in October and November. The leathery skin, which gets hard and firm during storage, keeps the inside of the fruit fresh and juicy. Therefore, the fruit can be stored several days at home without drying out. In the refrigerator, they can last up to three months.

CHARACTERISTICS

The juice contains tannic acid, which causes stains that are almost impossible to remove. The pomegranate is about 35% juice. The white seeds can be eaten if the fruit is eaten fresh.

TIPS ON HOW TO USE

The skins of fresh pomegranates are used in fruit salads and meat or fish dishes. The juice is squeezed out and processed to make ice cream, fruit juice beverages, sorbet, or jelly. When cooked with sugar, the juice turns into grenadine, which is used for cocktails.

PREPARATION

1. To extract the juice, cut the fruit into halves, and carefully squeeze it against a citrus press. Then pass the juice through a sieve to remove the remaining skin pieces.

2. To get out the individual seeds with skins, cut a large groove into the calyx of the fruit with a serrated knife and break the fruit into two halves.

3. Press out the seeds with skins over a bowl with a slight pressure on the skin. Remove the white skin, because it contains undesirable bitter substances.

Pomelo

ORIGIN

The pomelo (or shaddock), an ancient ancestor of the grapefruit, originated in the Malaysia-Indochina region. Today it is also grown in Israel, South Africa, Thailand, China, and Japan, though it is not grown on a large scale anywhere.

DESCRIPTION AND TASTE

The pomelo is larger than the grapefruit. The roundish fruit is surrounded by a thick, yellow-to-light green skin with large pores. The pulp is firm, light yellow and pink, and tastes quite sour. The white skin attached to the pulp contains bitter substances and should, if possible, be completely removed when the fruit is peeled.

PURCHASE AND STORAGE

Though they are difficult to find in the U.S., look for pomelos in Oriental markets from mid-January through mid-February. The fruit is ripe when the skin dents when slightly pressed with a finger. A slightly crumpled skin also indicates ripeness.

CHARACTERISTICS

Pomelos contain less vitamin C and minerals than grapefruits and have a very high content of tannic acid. Therefore be careful when you handle pomelos, as stains are difficult to remove.

TIPS ON HOW TO USE

Pomelos are eaten fresh, even though the pulp is much drier and more sour than that of the grapefruit. Otherwise, they are used like grapefruits (see page 39). The skin of organically grown pomelos is commonly candied and is quite delicious in that form.

PREPARATION

The pomelo is prepared like the grapefruit (see page 20).

Quince

ORIGIN

The quince is a native of Asia. Today, it is also grown on Crete, in Japan, North America, Spain, Italy, North Africa, and on the Balkan Peninsula. Most of our supply in the United States comes from California.

DESCRIPTION AND TASTE

Quinces are fruits of a high tree or shrub that is up to 20 feet high (6 m). The tree, like that of the pear and the apple, blossoms in the spring and bears fruit in the fall. Their leathery skin is light green-to-golden-yellow and is covered with a fine fluff. The ripe fruits give off a fresh scent much like a lemon, and they can weigh up to 2½ pounds (1.1 kg). The core contains red-brown pits, which have a bitter, almondlike flavor. Quinces are distinguished by their shape:
Apple quinces usually have a reddish, firm, woody pulp which is interspersed with seeds.
Pear or pineapple quinces are soft, aromatic, and produce a light red juice.

PURCHASE AND STORAGE

Quinces are harvested from September until November—for the most part only after the first frost—though they are sometimes available at other times of the year. Quinces do not ripen after they are picked and are very sensitive to pressure. Look for firm, unbruised, yellow-skinned fruit.

CHARACTERISTICS

Because of their strong scent, quinces can influence the taste of other foods when stored with them.

TIPS ON HOW TO USE

Cooked quinces taste pleasantly tart, somewhat like pineapples. They are too astringent and sour to be eaten raw. Because of their high pectin levels, they are often processed to make quince marmalade or jam. They are suitable for making stewed fruits, juice, ice cream, and wine, as well as fillings for cakes.

PREPARATION

Quinces are prepared just like apples and pears (see page 7).

Rambutan

ORIGIN

The rambutan is a purely tropical fruit that comes from Malaysia. It is also grown in Indonesia, Thailand, Southern India, Sri Lanka, and the Philippines.

DESCRIPTION AND TASTE

Rambut is the Malayan word for "hairy." Rambutans are related to lychees and grow, hanging together in clusters, on 49- to 65-feet-high (15 to 20 m) evergreen trees. The fruits are about the size of plums and have a parchment-like, red skin, which is divided into sections. The skin of the rambutan has long, wooly, soft or bristly, red, white, or yellow hairs. The pulp, which tastes like grapes and lemons, is white and tastes sweet-ish-sour. The fruit contains a long, inedible pit, which is hard to remove.

PURCHASE AND STORAGE

Rambutans can be stored at 41 to 50°F (5 to 10° C) for one to two weeks. From Malaysia and Thailand, rambutans come to us in cans.

TIPS ON HOW TO USE

The rambutan can be eaten fresh. It is also used in fruit salads, sauces for meat, fish, and poultry dishes, desserts, stewed fruits, ice cream, marmalade, cocktails, and mixed drinks.

PREPARATION

1. Either tear the skin open with your fingers or cut it open with a knife. Remove the skin.

2. Cut into the pulp up to the stone, pull the two halves apart, and remove the pit.

Raspberry

ORIGIN

Raspberries grow wild in the cooler regions of the Northern Hemisphere and in some southern parts. Though raspberries come from just one species, in North America we have the red raspberry, the eastern black raspberry, and the western black raspberry.

DESCRIPTION AND TASTE

The berries are red or black, very juicy, and have a extraordinary aroma. There are also some pink or yellow varieties, which are not sold commercially but grown primarily by recreational gardeners.

PURCHASE AND STORAGE

The harvesting and selling of raspberries takes place in the United States from mid-June through August. Imports from foreign countries can be found throughout the year. The berries are sensitive to pressure but can be stored in the refrigerator for several days. They are easy to freeze and are often sold frozen.

TIPS ON HOW TO USE

Raspberries are often eaten fresh or in combination with dairy products. In addition, they are used in desserts, fruit salads, ice cream, sorbet, marmalade, jelly, cakes and torts, vinegar, juice, wine, liqueur, and raspberry brandy.

PREPARATION

Select the berries and wash them well.

Star Fruit

ORIGIN

The star fruit, also called carambole, probably originated in Southeast Asia, India, and Malaysia. Today, it is widespread throughout the tropics and subtropics.

DESCRIPTION AND TASTE

Star fruits are the fruits of a small tree that needs a tropical, humid, and warm climate. After four years, the tree bears fruit for the first time. The fruit ranges from 2¼ to 4¾ inches long (6 to 12 cm) and has five to six longitudinal grooves. When the fruit is cut crosswise, it forms star-shaped slices—thus, its name. There are two types of star fruit. The larger one is golden yellow and smells somewhat of jasmine. It tastes sweet and is very aromatic. The smaller variety is light yellow-to-green and tastes sour.

PURCHASE AND STORAGE

Star fruit is available in the United States throughout the year. For transport, they are wrapped individually in paper and packed into crates. The fruits can be stored for a short time at 47 to 50°F (8 to 10°C), but there is the danger that the edges will turn brown.

TIPS ON HOW TO USE

The star fruit can be eaten fresh, like an apple, but it is also used as a decorative trimming for drinks, fruit salads, desserts, pies, appetizers, and entrees.

PREPARATION

1. Should the edges of the star fruit develop brown spots, simply cut the spots off with a small knife.

2. Then cut the fruit (with the skins on) into slices crosswise.

Tamarillo

ORIGIN

Tamarillos, also called tree tomatoes, come from the Peruvian Andes. Today, they are grown in New Zealand, Brazil, Ecuador, Columbia, Kenya, California, Sri Lanka, and India, as well as on Java and Madeira.

DESCRIPTION AND TASTE

The tamarillo belongs, like the tomato, to the Solanaceae family and very much resembles it in appearance but not taste. Tamarillos grow, hanging together on long stems, on 20-feet-high (6 m) evergreen trees. The egg-shaped fruits have a yellow, orange, red, or brown-red thin skin and weigh approximately $2\frac{1}{4}$ to $2\frac{1}{2}$ ounces (70 to 80 g). The yellow-to-red pulp contains a jellylike substance filled with many inedible, soft, dark pits. Tamarillos have a pleasantly bitter taste.

PURCHASE AND STORAGE

Tamarillos are sold fresh throughout the year, and whole, peeled fruits are available in cans. They are picked while they are not quite ripe and are very difficult to transport.

Strawberry

ORIGIN

The strawberry originated in America and is now grown in almost all countries of the world. Due to different methods of cultivation, it grows in subtropical as well as arctic regions.

DESCRIPTION AND TASTE

Strawberries are known as false fruits. We refer to the blossom bottom, on which small, slightly sunken nuts are sitting, as the fruit, when in fact the nuts are the actual fruits. The shapes and sizes of the over 1,000 varieties differ greatly; the color ranges from light to dark red. The smaller the berries, the sweeter and more intense their taste. The wild-growing wood strawberries have the strongest flavor.

PURCHASE AND STORAGE

Strawberries are sold throughout the year. Unblemished fruits last for a couple of days in the refrigerator. Strawberries are very sensitive to pressure and should therefore be stored next to each other—not on top of each other.

TIPS ON HOW TO USE

The strawberry is usually eaten fresh. But it is also processed to make marmalade, jelly, stewed fruits, or (combined with other fruits) syrup, and fruit wine.

PREPARATION

Pull off the leaves and wash the berries well.

TIPS ON HOW TO USE

Tamarillos can be eaten uncooked without the skin. But they also go well cooked with meat, poultry, and fish dishes, particularly shellfish.

PREPARATION

1. Peel uncooked tamarillos with a knife or with a peeler.

2. You can aslo carve tamarillos crosswise, pour boiling water over them, put them into cold water, and take off the skin.

3. After they are peeled, cut out the stem, then cut them—like tomatoes—into slices or pieces or puree.

Tangerine

ORIGIN

Tangerines belong to the citrus family. They originated in China but are today also cultivated in most Mediterranean countries, South America, South Africa, Australia, and the United States.

DESCRIPTION AND TASTE

Tangerines grow either on shrubs or on 13- to 20-feet-high (4 to 6 m) evergreen trees. They are small fruits that look much like an orange. They have a thin, orange-colored skin which is loosely sitting on the pulp and which can be easily peeled by hand. The pulp is divided into 8 to 12 chambers or segments, which are easily separated. While most varieties contain pits, some do not. The pulp is firm, juicy, and tastes sweetish-sour. Tangerines are the sweetest of the citrus fruits.

PURCHASE AND STORAGE

Tangerines are available from the beginning of October through the winter months. The fruit can be eaten when the skin is green and speckled. At a temperature of 43 to 47°F (6 to 8°C), they can be stored for up to six weeks.

TIPS ON HOW TO USE

Tangerines are usually eaten fresh, though they can also be processed to make jam, candied fruits, sweets, liqueur, and other beverages.

PREPARATION

Little need be said about the peeling and processing of the tangerine, because it has most certainly been taught to each of us while we were young.

Watermelon

ORIGIN

The watermelon comes from South and Central Africa and there, because of its high water content (93%), it serves as a substitute for drinking water. Today, it is cultivated primarily in Southern Europe, Egypt, the South of the former USSR, the United States, South America, Japan, and China.

DESCRIPTION AND TASTE

The large, elongated round fruit can weigh up to 33 pounds (15 kg). The skin is smooth, thick, light-to-dark green, and striped or marbleized. The red, firm pulp contains numerous dark pits and tastes very sweet and slightly watery.

PURCHASE AND STORAGE

Watermelons are sold by their weight, and melons that weigh around 5½ pounds (2.5 kg) are preferred for export. In the U.S., they are available in the summer months. The ripeness of the melon can be checked by knocking on the skin. When it "sings," it is ripe. Melons are also sold in pieces, wrapped in plastic, and can be stored for several days in the refrigerator.

TIPS ON HOW TO USE

Watermelons are eaten fresh and are also suitable in fruit salads, cold soups, sorbets, and desserts. In addition, they go well with salty foods like cold cuts, cheese, fish, and meat.

PREPARATION

1. Cut the melon with a large knife into slices.

2. Remove the pits individually with a fork.

Beef Stock

Makes about 5 cups (1¼ l)

4 pounds (2.5 kg) meaty beef bones (shank, neck bones, etc.), sawed into 2-inch (5 cm) pieces

¼ cup (80 ml) vegetable oil

3 cups (500 g) onions, cut into large chunks

3 or 4 medium carrots, peeled and cut into large chunks

3 or 4 celery stalks, cut into large chunks

1½ tablespoons tomato paste

6 cups (1½ l) dry red wine

10 to 12 peppercorns

2 bay leaves

4 whole cloves

2 sprigs fresh thyme, finely chopped or 1 tablespoon dried thyme

1 clove garlic, coarsely chopped

1. Preheat the oven to 350°F. (177°C). Pour the vegetable oil into a shallow roasting pan, and add the bones. Roast them in the oven, turning them frequently.

2. When the bones are golden brown all over, add the vegetables and return the pan to the oven for 15 minutes. Pour the fat out of the pan and stir in the tomato paste. Return the pan to the oven and bake until the paste roasts dry. Then, add the red wine. Let everything cook again, until the tomato paste roasts dry again.

3. Cover the bones with cold water and loosen the dried gravy with a spatula. Transfer everything into a large pot and bring to a boil on the stove.

4. After the liquid has come to a boil, skim off the foam for about 5 minutes. Add all the spices, herbs, and garlic, and cook on very low heat for 1 to 1½ hours. Remove the bones and vegetables and discard. Strain the stock into a pot through a fine cheesecloth.

5. Cook the stock on very low heat until it's reduced by two-thirds. Degrease the stock by blotting it with a paper towel.

6. To store the stock, pour it hot into sterile glass containers or freeze it in plastic containers. Tightly covered, the stock can be stored for up to five days in the refrigerator.

Chicken Stock

Makes about 5 cups (1¼ l)

3 pounds soup or stew chicken, washed and ready to cook

1 onion, cut in half

2 medium carrots, peeled and cut into chunks

1 cup (80 g) leeks, well cleaned and coarsely chopped

stems from 1 bunch of fresh parsley

2 stalks of celery, cut into chunks

½ clove of garlic, coarsely chopped

1 bay leaf

1 whole clove

1. Place the chicken into a deep pot and add enough cold water to cover. Bring the chicken to a boil and skim off the foam for about 5 minutes. Then, simmer over low heat for 1 hour.

2. In a skillet, roast the onion halves until their cut surfaces are dark brown. Add them to the pot along with the other vegetables and the spices. Cook the mixture over moderate heat for 1½ hours.

3. Remove the chicken and vegetables and discard. Strain the liquid into a pot through a fine cheesecloth. Degrease the stock by blotting it with a paper towel.

4. To store the stock, pour it hot into sterile glass containers or freeze it in small plastic containers. Tightly covered, the stock can be stored for up to five days in the refrigerator.

Fish Stock

Makes about 5 cups (1¼ l)

2 pounds (1 kg) fish bones and heads of white-fleshed, nonoily fish (pike, flounder, sole, wea fish, turbot, etc.), washed and cut into pieces
3 to 4 shallots, cut into thin rings
½ fennel bulb, cut into thin strips
½ celery stalk, cut into thin strips
¼ cup (50 ml) olive oil
2 cups (½ l) dry white wine

1 bay leaf
2 whole cloves
6 to 8 peppercorns
2 sprigs of fresh thyme chopped coarsely or 1 teaspoon dried thyme

1. In a large pot, sauté the shallots in oil until translucent. Then, lightly sauté the fennel and celery.

2. Add the fish bones to the vegetables. Stir once and then add the white wine. Add enough water to cover the bones. Add the spices and the thyme.

3. Slowly bring the stock to a boil over moderate heat. Skim off the foam for 5 minutes and let the stock simmer over very low heat for 20 minutes.

4. Remove the fish bones and the vegetables and discard. Strain the liquid into a pot through a fine cheesecloth. To store the stock, pour it hot into sterile glass containers or freeze it in small plastic containers.

Crème Fraîche

Makes 2 cups

1 cup (250 g) heavy cream (not ultrapasteurized)
1 cup (200 g) sour cream

1. Whisk heavy cream and sour cream together in a bowl. Loosely cover with plastic wrap and let stand in the kitchen or other fairly warm area overnight or until thickened. In cold weather this may take up to 24 hours.

2. Place the covered bowl in the refrigerator for at least 4 hours or until the crème fraîche becomes very thick. The tart flavor will become more pronounced as the crème fraîche sits in the refrigerator.

Purified Sugar

Makes 1¾ cups (400 ml)

1¼ cups (250 g) granulated sugar
1 cup (¼ l) water

1. Combine the sugar and the water in a pot and bring to a boil over medium heat, stirring continuously with a whisk. Let the mixture boil for about 1 minute or until it reaches a syrupy consistency. Then remove the pot from the stove.

2. Pour the syrup hot into bottles or glasses. Stored in this way, the purified sugar will keep for a long period of time.

Appetizers and Soups

Fruits are most often used in preparing desserts. But recently a wide range of common and exotic fruits—some with very distinctive tastes—have been starring in or playing complementary roles in all kinds of dishes, including appetizers, salads, and soups like those presented in this chapter.

Avocado Orange Salad with Raspberry Vinaigrette

A perfect salad year 'round, you'll be happy to make this one again and again.

∽

Makes 4 servings
FOR THE SALAD
2 ripe avocados
juice from ½ lemon
3 oranges
1 small head of curly lettuce
2 tablespoons roasted sunflower seeds

FOR THE VINAIGRETTE
4 tablespoons raspberry vinegar
pinch of salt
¼ teaspoon coarsely ground black pepper
6 tablespoons olive oil

1. Peel the avocados, cut them into halves, and remove the pits. Cut the avocados into slices, as shown in the photograph. Trickle lemon juice onto the slices.
2. Peel the oranges and cut out the segments, as described on page 31. Squeeze the juice from the fruit walls into a bowl. Break the curly lettuce into pieces.
3. Add the raspberry vinegar to the orange juice, stir in the salt and pepper, and mix in the oil. Blend in 2 tablespoons of water.
4. Arrange the lettuce in a spiral fashion on plates. Place the avocado slices and the orange segments in the center, using the photo as a guide. Drizzle the vinaigrette over everything. Finally, sprinkle the roasted sunflower seeds on top.

Pears and Grapefruit Salad with Cooked Ham

The sharp flavors of grapefruit and endive are nicely balanced by sweet pears and cream.

∽

Makes 4 servings
2 pears
juice from ½ lemon
3 tablespoons Crème Fraîche (page 47)
1 tablespoon confectioners' sugar
1 tablespoon pear liqueur
salt and white pepper to taste
2 pink grapefruits
2 heads of endive
4 slices of cooked ham
4 sprigs of fresh chervil or parsley

1. Peel the pears, cut them into 4 pieces, and cut out the cores. Cut the quarters first into slices, then into ¼-inch-wide (0.6 cm) strips. Put these in a bowl and trickle lemon juice over them.
2. Put the crème fraîche into a bowl, sift in the confectioners' sugar, and stir until smooth. Blend in the pear liqueur and lightly season with salt and pepper. Pour the sauce over the pears and carefully blend.
3. Peel the grapefruits and cut them into segments (see page 21).
4. Peel off the endive leaves. Clean and dry them with a paper towel, then cut them into halves lengthwise. Place the endives in a half circle on the plates and place a dollop of pear salad in the center. Add the grapefruit segments as shown in the photo and place 1 slice of ham on each plate. Garnish the salad with chervil or parsley.

Calf's Tongue and Tangerine Salad with Lemon Balm Vinaigrette

This tangy salad tastes just as good with smoked ham.

∽

Makes 4 servings
8 medium tangerines, peeled
dash of powdered ginger
1 pickled, cooked calf's tongue
some drops of Tabasco sauce
pinch of salt
⅓ cup (100 ml) sunflower oil
1 small bunch of lemon balm, finely chopped
salad leaves, for garnishing

1. Cut out the segments from 6 tangerines (see page 31). Squeeze the juice from the fruit walls into a pot. Add the juice from the other 2 tangerines.
2. Bring the tangerine juice to a boil, add the ginger, and reduce the liquid by half. Let it cool.
3. Using a cutting machine or sharp knife, cut the tongue lengthwise into thin slices.
4. Season with Tabasco and salt to taste. Blend in the oil. Add the lemon balm.
5. Arrange the tongue slices and tangerine segments on plates, garnish with the salad leaves, and pour the vinaigrette over everything.

Pickled Salmon with Grapefruit and Green Asparagus

The marinated salmon melts in your mouth and tastes great with the grapefruit and fresh asparagus.

Marinating time: 24 hours
Makes 4 servings
18 ounces (500 g) salmon fillet, center piece, bones removed, with skin

FOR THE PICKLING MARINADE
4 teaspoons salt
1 tablespoon granulated sugar
1 tablespoon mustard seeds
1 tablespoon black peppercorns
1 whole clove
2 bundles of dill, finely cut

FOR THE SALAD
1 pound (500 g) green asparagus
¼ teaspoon salt
juice of ½ lemon
¼ teaspoon granulated sugar
1 white grapefruit
1 pink grapefruit
3 tablespoons raspberry vinegar
pepper to taste
6 tablespoons vegetable oil
some lettuce for garnishing

1. For the pickling marinade, mix the salt and sugar in a bowl. Crush the mustard seeds, peppercorns, and clove with a mortar in a pestle and add to the bowl.
2. Place the salmon, skin side down, on a deep tray and spread the marinade over it. Add the dill and cover the fish with plastic wrap. Marinate the fish in the refrigerator for 12 hours, then turn it over and marinate for another 12 hours.
3. Cut off the light ends of the asparagus stalks. Cut the stalks into 3-inch (7.5 cm) pieces. Place them in a pot to which you have added enough water to cover the vegetables, the salt, lemon juice, and sugar; cook for 10 minutes. Remove the asparagus and chill. Save the asparagus stock.
4. Peel the grapefruits, take out the segments (see page 21), and squeeze the juice from the fruit walls into a bowl. Mix the juice with the raspberry vinegar, add salt and pepper to taste, and blend in the oil. Finally, stir in 2 to 3 tablespoons of asparagus stock.
5. Remove the salmon from the marinade and cut the fillet into even, paper-thin slices.
6. Place the asparagus, the grapefruit sections, and the lettuce leaves in a bowl and toss with the vinaigrette. Arrange everything, including the salmon slices, on plates.

Smoked Salmon Rosettes with Pomegranate Jelly

This unusual and savory salad will certainly impress guests.

Makes 4 servings
FOR THE JELLY
1 teaspoon of unflavored gelatine·
2 pomegranates
1 tablespoon granulated sugar
1 cup (¼ l) dry white wine

FOR THE SALAD
½ cup (⅛ l) heavy cream
juice of ½ lemon
20 very thin slices of smoked salmon
some creasy greens
salt and white pepper to taste
1 tablespoon coarse mustard

1. Halve the pomegranates and squeeze out the juice with a hand juicer. Put the juice into a pot and add the sugar and white wine. Bring the liquid to a boil and reduce over low heat to 1 cup (¼ l).

2. Pour the pomegranate juice through a strainer. Add gelatine and dissolve it in the still hot, but not boiling, liquid. Pour the liquid into a small bowl and let it harden in the refrigerator for 30 minutes: it will gel part way.

3. Pour the heavy cream into a bowl, mix in the lemon juice, and let sit.

4. Twist the smoked salmon slices into rosettes and arrange them in a circle on plates. Garnish with the creasy greens.

5. Season the heavy cream with salt, pepper, and mustard. Spoon the pomegranate jelly onto the middle of each plate and spoon the mustard sauce on the outside of the plate around the salmon rosettes.

Melon Balls in Port Sauce

This fabulous fruit salad has an unforgettable taste and a very pleasing presentation.

Makes 4 servings
4 small cantaloupes
½ cup (⅛ l) red port (divided)
1 tablespoon granulated sugar
¼ teaspoon powdered ginger
pinch of salt
2 limes
small bundle of fresh peppermint, finely cut into strips

1. Cut each of the melons down the center in a zig-zag fashion. Separate the 2 halves by twisting them. Remove the seeds.
2. Using a melon baller, scoop out 6 to 8 melon balls from each of the 8 halves. Put the balls in a bowl and pour half the port over them.
3. Scrape out the remaining fruit with a spoon. Put the sugar into a pot and heat until it caramelizes. Add the rest of the port and chill. To the chilled mixture, add the scraped out melon, the ginger, and the salt. Warm up everything for 5 minutes. Puree this port sauce in a processor and let cool.
4. Wash the lime with hot water and cut it into thin slices. Let the marinated melon balls drain into a bowl. Fill each of the 8 empty melon halves with melon balls. Add the drained port to the port sauce and blend.
5. Place the lime slices along the outer edge of the melons. Pour the port sauce over everything and garnish with mint.

Prosciutto with Pears and Figs

This wonderful salad captures the romance and flavors of summer in Italy.

Marinating time: 6 hours
Makes 4 servings
6 figs
4 tablespoons vodka
½ cup (⅛ l) Purified Sugar (page 47)
½ cup (⅛ l) dry white wine
4 pears
juice of ½ lemon
2 tablespoons Crème Fraîche (page 47)
some lettuce leaves for garnishing
12 thin slices of prosciutto
4 stems of fresh peppermint

1. Peel the figs (see page 18) and prick them with a needle several times all around. Place them on a platter.
2. Combine the vodka, ⅓ cup (100 ml) of purified sugar, and the white wine in a pot and bring to a boil over moderate heat. Let the mixture cool a little and then pour it over the figs. Cover the platter of figs with plastic wrap and marinate the figs for 6 hours in the refrigerator.
3. Peel the pears, cut them into quarters, and remove the cores. First cut the pears into slices and then into fine strips. Put the pears in a bowl and trickle the lemon juice over them. Mix the remaining purified sugar with the crème fraîche and blend it into the pears.
4. Take the figs out of the marinade, let them drain, and cut them into quarters. Arrange the pears, lettuce, pear salad, prosciutto, and figs as shown in the photo and garnish with mint.

Roast Beef with Mustard Fruits

Once you try these delectable marinated fruits, you'll want to keep several jars on hand year 'round.

Marinating Time: 2 days
Cooking and cooling the beef:
3 to 4 hours
Makes 8 servings

FOR THE MUSTARD FRUITS
2 cups (425 g) granulated sugar (divided)
1 firm mango
1 papaya
1 pineapple
1 star fruit
2 nashis
2 limes
2/3 cup (157 ml) white wine vinegar
3 tablespoons powdered mustard

FOR THE SALAD
3 pounds (1.5 kg) roast beef
salt and pepper to taste
seasonal salad leaves in season, for garnishing

Prepare the mustard fruits 2 days before you serve them. To do so, combine in a pot 1 1/3 cups (280 g) of sugar with 1/2 cup (1/8 l) of water and bring to boil. Simmer over low heat for 10 to 15 minutes. 2. Peel the mango, halve it, remove the stone (see page 26), and cut the fruit into 1/4-inch-thick (1 cm) slices. Peel the papaya, halve it, take out the seeds (see page 32), and cut the fruit into 1/4-inch-thick (1 cm) slices. Peel the pineap- ple, cut it into quarters, remove the stalk (see page 37), and cube the fruit. Cut the star fruit into slices. Wash the nashis, halve them, cut out the cores, and cut the fruit into slices. Wash the limes and cut them into thin slices.

3. Add the fruits to the sugared water according to how long each needs to cook; begin with the limes, then the pineapple, then the mango and papaya, and last the star fruit and nashis. Cook until soft, then remove the pot from the stove.

4. Combine the remaining 2/3 cup (145 g) of sugar with the vinegar and boil it down to a syrup. Stir in the powdered mustard and pour this mixture over the cooked fruits.

5. Put the hot mustard fruits into sterile glass containers and seal. Let marinate for 2 days. Unopened, the mustard fruits will last for 5 to 6 months.

6. To roast the beef: Preheat the oven to 425°F (218.3°C). Season the meat with salt and pepper, place on a roasting pan, and cook in the preheated oven for 10 minutes; then cook for another 35 minutes at 325°F (162.8°C). In between, baste with the beef juices. Cook until the meat thermometer registers between 140 and 150°F (60 and 65°C); the cooked roast beef should be pink.

7. Wrap the cooked meat in aluminum foil and let it cool for 2 to 3 hours.

8. Cut the cooled roast beef into thin slices, place these fanlike onto the plates, and serve with the salad leaves. Spoon 3 tablespoons of mustard fruits onto each plate.

Spring Rolls with Papaya

These vegetarian spring rolls are bursting with flavor.

⌣

Makes 4 servings
FOR THE SPRING ROLLS
2 medium carrots, cut into fine strips
2 small celery stalks, cut into fine strips
1 cup (100 g) leeks, well cleaned and cut into thin rings
1 small papaya
2 cups (200 g) bean sprouts
½ clove of garlic, chopped
3 tablespoons peanut oil
salt and white pepper to taste
10 tablespoons soy sauce (divided)
1 teaspoon cornstarch
1 tablespoon finely cut lemon balm
8 sheets of egg roll dough
1 tablespoon all-purpose flour
peanut oil for deep frying

⌣

1. Peel the papaya, take out the seeds, and cut into thin strips (see page 32).
2. Heat 3 tablespoons of oil in a frying pan or wok until very hot. Add the garlic, the cut vegetables, and the papaya strips and season everything with salt and pepper. Stir-fry this mixture over high heat for 3 minutes. Add 3 tablespoons of soy sauce and stir-fry for 5 minutes or until the vegetables are soft enough to bite into: do not overcook!
3. Dissolve the cornstarch in cold water and pour over the cooked mixture to thicken the sauce. Put the mixture on a plate and let it cool. Then stir in the lemon balm.
4. In a cup, mix the flour with 1 tablespoon of cold water. Then stir in 2 to 3 tablespoons of hot water.

5. Place the dough sheets on a moist cloth and spread the vegetable-papaya mixture onto them. Brush the edges of the sheets with the flour paste and roll the dough sheets together. To do so, fold the sides into the middle and then roll everything together. Slightly press each roll so that the seams are tightly sealed.
6. Heat some peanut oil until very hot and deep-fry the spring rolls until golden brown. Drain them on paper towels and serve with the remaining soy sauce as a dipping sauce.

Sliced Raw Beef with Avocado and Olive Vinaigrette

To ensure success with this remarkable salad, be sure to buy the finest and freshest beef you can find.

❧

Makes 4 servings
FOR THE VINAIGRETTE
15 to 20 large black olives
3 tablespoons balsamic vinegar
salt and coarsely ground black pepper to taste
9 tablespoons cold-pressed olive oil

FOR THE SALAD
2 avocados
salt and pepper to taste
juice from 1 lemon
14 ounces (400 g) beef fillet, sliced and pounded paper thin
3 tablespoons roasted pine nuts
1 small bundle of fresh chervil or smooth parsley, coarsely chopped

❧

1. Remove the pits from the olives and cut the olives into strips. Put them in a bowl and add the balsamic vinegar. Add salt and pepper and blend in the olive oil.
2. Peel the avocados, halve them, take out the stones (see page 9), and cut the pulp into thin slices. Season with salt and pepper and trickle the lemon juice over them.

3. Arrange the avocado slices and the raw beef slices in a circle on plates. Drizzle with vinaigrette and sprinkle pine nuts over everything. Garnish with herbs.

Chicken Liver Paté with Fig Confit

Launch a special winter meal with this rich appetizer, and toast your guests with a glass of smooth, red wine.

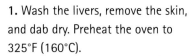

Makes 8 servings
FOR THE PATÉ
7½ ounces (220 g) chicken liver
8 ounces (220 g) sweet butter
8 tablespoons red port
8 tablespoons Madeira
1 egg
1 egg yolk
salt and freshly ground white pepper to taste
pinch of ground nutmeg
butter for the aluminum foil

FOR THE FIG CONFIT
10 fresh figs

2 tablespoons red port
½ cup (⅛ l) red wine
dash of ground ginger
peppermint for garnishing

1. Wash the livers, remove the skin, and dab dry. Preheat the oven to 325°F (160°C).
2. Melt the butter, bring it to a boil, and let it simmer over low heat until golden brown.
3. Combine the red wine and the port in a pot over moderate heat and let it reduce to about one-third.
4. Puree the livers, the egg, and the egg yolk in a food processor. Pass the lukewarm butter through a strainer and let it run in a thin stream onto the liver mixture. Season with salt, pepper, and nutmeg.
5. Add the spirits and pass the paté mixture through a strainer.

6. Line a bread loaf pan with aluminum foil, leaving enough on all sides so that the foil can cover the top of the paté. Grease the foil with butter. Pour the paté mixture into the pan and fold the foil over the top. Place the pan into another baking dish, filled with warm water up to two fingers below the edge.
7. Cook the paté in the oven for 25 to 30 minutes. Then, let it cool.
8. For the fig confit, peel the figs (see page 18), and slice them. Put the fruit into a pot and bring it to a boil with the sugar, port, and red wine. Cook over low heat until the fruit preserves thicken. Then, season with ginger and pass through a strainer. Let cool.
9. Take the paté out of the loaf pan, remove the aluminum foil, and cut the paté into slices. Serve with the fig confit and garnish with peppermint.

Salmon Fillet with Rambutan Vinaigrette

Serve this gorgeous appetizer lukewarm to enhance its melt-in-your mouth taste.

Makes 4 servings

FOR THE VINAIGRETTE

16 rambutans (or lychees)

4 tablespoons apple-cider vinegar

salt and white pepper to taste

6 tablespoons grape-pit oil

1 tablespoon minced chives

some drops of lemon juice

FOR THE SALAD

2 bunches of yellow endive

2 bunches of red endive or radicchio

4 salmon fillets, 3 to 4 ounces (100 g) each, bones and skin removed

2 shallots, minced

1 tablespoon sweet butter

salt and white pepper to taste

½ cup (⅛ liter) dry white wine

½ cup (⅛ liter) Fish Stock (page 47)

1. Peel the rambutans, halve them, and remove the pits (see page 41). Put them aside.

2. Mix the vinegar with the salt and pepper and blend in the oil. Add the minced chives and season the vinaigrette with some lemon juice.

3. Grease a deep baking dish with butter and line the pan with shallots. Season the salmon fillets with salt and pepper and place them on top of the shallots.

4. Combine the white wine with the fish stock and pour the mixture over the fillets. Cover the baking dish with aluminum foil and bake in the oven at 350° F (177° C) for 6 to 8 minutes.

5. Arrange the salad in a circle on 4 plates. Stir another 2 to 3 tablespoons of the fish stock into the vinaigrette and trickle half of it over the salad. Pour the other half over the rambutans.

6. Take the salmon fillets out of the dish, let them drain, and arrange them on the salad. Pour the rambutan vinaigrette over them.

Avocado Buttermilk Soup with Salmon Cakes

Here's a rich, creamy soup that makes a satisfying appetizer or a light meal.

Makes 4 Servings

FOR THE SOUP

2 medium avocados

juice from 1 lemon

⅔ cup (150 ml) Chicken Stock (page 46) or canned chicken broth

1¼ cups (300 ml) buttermilk

pinch of salt

some drops of Tabasco sauce

chopped fresh herbs such as chervil, dill, or tarragon

FOR THE SALMON CAKES

9 ounces (250 g) salmon fillet, bones and skin removed

2 small, sweet pickles, cut into small cubes

1 teaspoon capers, finely chopped

1 shallot, minced

salt and white pepper to taste

splash of lemon

1 egg yolk

1 tablespoon sweet butter

1. Halve the avocados, remove the stones (see page 9), and scoop out the pulp with a spoon. Trickle the lemon juice on the fruit and cut it into pieces.

2. Put the chicken stock and the avocado pieces in a food processor. Puree everything, pour the mixture into a bowl, and stir in the buttermilk with a whisk. Season the soup with salt and Tabasco and let it cool.

3. In the meantime, cut the salmon into small cubes and chop it finely with a large, heavy kitchen knife. Put the fish into a bowl.

4. Add the pickles, capers, and shallots. Season with salt, pepper, and lemon juice. Stir in the egg yolk and form 4 cakes of equal size.

5. Melt the butter in a large skillet and briefly cook the salmon cakes on both sides. Divide the avocado soup into 4 bowls. Place a salmon cake in each bowl and garnish the soup with herbs.

Creamed Melon Soup

*Potatoes and melon may seem
an odd pairing, but blended
together they create a
surprisingly delicious soup.*

Makes 4 servings
3 to 4 medium white potatoes
1 honeydew melon or cantaloupe
2 cups (½ l) milk (divided)
1½ tablespoons sweet butter
salt and white pepper to taste
3 egg yolks
4 tablespoons sour cream
4 fresh peppermint leaves

1. Peel and wash the potatoes, cut them into cubes, and cook them in plenty of water until soft. Then pour out the water and let them steam off.

2. In the meantime, halve the melon and remove the seeds. Scoop out the pulp with a spoon.

3. Combine the lukewarm potatoes, the melon, and ⅔ cup (160 ml) milk in a food processor, and puree.

4. Melt the butter in a pot and add it to the purée along with the remaining milk. Let the soup simmer over low heat for about 5 minutes. Season with salt and pepper.

5. Whisk the yolks and add them to the simmering soup, stirring constantly. Let the soup simmer for another 5 minutes: do not let it boil. Serve the soup in deep bowls. Put 1 tablespoon of sour cream and 1 mint leaf in the middle of each bowl.

Lemon Soup

This tangy variation of chicken
and rice soup tastes terrific
on a cold day.

Makes 4 servings

6 cups (1.5 liter) Chicken Stock
(page 46) or canned chicken broth
2 cups (80 g) long-grain white rice
2 organic lemons
3 egg yolks
salt
some drops of Tabasco sauce
2 stems of fresh peppermint or
lemon balm, cut into fine strips

1. Bring the chicken stock to a boil
in a pot. Add the rice and let it
cook over moderate heat for 15 to
18 minutes.

2. In the meantime, grate the skin
of 1 lemon and add it to the soup.
Peel the rest of the lemon and cut
out the segments (see page 23).
Squeeze the juice from the second
lemon into a bowl.

3. When the rice is done, whisk
together the lemon juice and the
egg yolks, and stir 5 to 6 tablespoons into the soup. Add the rest
of the egg yolks, stirring constantly. Simmer the soup for 5
minutes—do not let it boil.

4. Remove the pot from the stove,
season with salt and Tabasco, and
add the lemon segments. Add the
mint or lemon balm. Serve the
soup hot.

Orange Carrot Soup

To make a sensational meal of this soup, add cooked shrimp or crab meat and serve with fresh bread.

Makes: 4 servings

5 to 6 medium carrots, sliced
2 medium onions, chopped
2 tablespoons sweet butter
salt and white pepper to taste
4 cups (1 l) Chicken Stock (page 46)
or canned chicken broth
1 organic orange
2 tablespoons granulated sugar
2 oranges
6 tablespoons heavy cream

1. Melt the butter in a pot, sauté the onions until transparent, and add the carrots. Season with salt and pepper and cook, covered with a lid, for about 5 minutes. Add the chicken stock and let the soup simmer for 10 minutes.
2. In the meantime, peel the rind of the organic orange with a zester (set the orange aside) and let the rind cook until tender in 1 cup (^{1}/$_4$ l) of water to which you've added 2 tablespoons of sugar. Then rinse off the zested rind with water, dab it dry, and set aside.
3. Squeeze all the oranges and combine the juice and the soup in a food processor and puree it thoroughly. Pass the soup through a strainer and heat it up again, but do not let it boil anymore. Season the soup with salt and pepper.

4. Blend the heavy cream into the soup, sprinkle it with the orange rinds, and serve it hot.

Hot Apple Soup

Celebrate autumn by inviting friends over to share a bowl of this lovely soup.

Makes 4 servings

^{1}/$_3$ cup (60 g) white rice
salt and white pepper to taste
2 medium tart apples
4 cups (1 l) Chicken Stock (page 46)
or canned chicken broth
^{1}/$_4$ teaspoon powdered ginger
2 tablespoons apple schnapps
(Calvados)

1. Cook the rice in plenty of water over moderate heat for 15 to 20 minutes. Drain the cooked rice and cool it with cold water.
2. In the meantime, peel the apples, cut them into quarters, and cut out the cores. Slice the apples and put them into a pot with the chicken stock. Bring everything to a boil over moderate heat, then let it simmer for about 15 minutes over low heat until the apples fall apart.
3. Use the back of a spoon to push the mixture through a strainer. Season it with powdered ginger and pepper.
4. Reheat the soup, add the apple schnapps, and let everything simmer for 5 minutes. Finally, add the rice to the soup.

Poultry and Meat

In this chapter, you will find a wide assortment of
recipes using a variety of fruits in delicious
combinations with chicken, beef, pork, ham,
turkey, lamb, and veal.

Chicken Breast with Curried Fruits and Grated Coconut

You can prepare this tasty meal with veal or pork. To turn up the heat, add a small chopped hot, green chili to the cooking meat.

❧

Makes 4 servings

8 rambutans or lychees

1 kiwi

2 loquats or apricots

1 banana

2 passion fruits

2 boneless chicken breasts without skin, 4–5 ounces (150 g) each

4 tablespoons vegetable oil

salt and white pepper to taste

2 tablespoons sweet butter

2 tablespoons grated coconut

1 tablespoon curry powder

dash of cayenne pepper or some drops of Tabasco

1 cup (¼ l) Chicken Stock (page 46) or canned chicken broth

1 teaspoon cornstarch

1 to 2 tablespoons sour cream or Crème Fraîche (page 47)

❧

1. Peel the rambutans or lychees, halve them, and remove the pits (see page 41 or page 25). Peel the kiwi, cut it in half, and then slice finely. Remove the skin from the loquats and slice them or wash the apricots, halve them, remove the pits (see page 8), and cut into slices. Halve the passion fruits, scrape out the fruit with a spoon, and pass it through a strainer.

2. Wash the chicken breasts and pat them dry. Cut them into ½-inch-wide (1.3 cm) strips. Heat the oil in a large skillet and sauté the strips over high heat until brown. Season with salt and pepper and cook another 1 to 2 minutes. Drain the chicken in a strainer placed over a bowl to catch the juices.

3. Blot the skillet with a paper towel. Melt 1½ tablespoons of butter. Place the prepared fruits, one after another (except for the passion fruit), into the butter, and fry them. Then place them with the chicken in the strainer.

4. Put the remaining ½ tablespoon of butter into the pan, sprinkle in the grated coconut, and briefly cook in the pan juices. Add the curry powder and the cayenne pepper or Tabasco and quench everything with passion fruit juice. Add the chicken stock, bring to a boil, and let the sauce simmer for 5 minutes.

5. Add to the sauce the juices that have drained from the chicken and the fruit. Mix the cornstarch with cold water, thicken the sauce with it, and again bring the sauce to a boil.

6. Reheat the chicken strips and the fruits in the sauce, but do not let it boil anymore. Shortly before you serve the dish, stir in the crème fraîche or sour cream. Serve with rice.

Chicken in Spicy Coconut Sauce

Warm Indian bread or pita bread go well with this easy-to-prepare curried chicken.

Marinating time: about 30 minutes
Makes 4 servings

3 pounds (1.5 kg) chicken, cut into 8 pieces, skin removed
1 tablespoon ground coriander
1 teaspoon ground chili
1 teaspoon turmeric powder
1 teaspoon ground black pepper
3 tablespoons grated coconut
5 tablespoons vegetable oil
4 medium potatoes, cut into bite-size cubes

1. Mix the spices and the grated coconut with 1 tablespoon oil and coat the poultry pieces with the mixture. Put the chicken pieces in a bowl and let them marinate for at least 30 minutes.

2. Heat up the remaining 4 table-spoons of oil in a large casserole pot and carefully brown the chicken on all sides. Add the potato cubes, brown them thouroughly, and remove them from the pot.

3. Add enough water to the pot to partially cover the chicken. Simmer the chicken for 30 to 35 minutes uncovered, turning the pieces several times.

4. When the chicken is done, add the potatoes, and season the sauce with the spices one more time. Serve the chicken with the sauce.

Lemon Chicken

Herbed rice goes well with this light and tangy meal.

Makes 4 servings

2 whole chickens, 1 ¾ to 2 ½ pounds (800 g) each

salt and pepper to taste

4 stems of fresh rosemary

6 to 8 shallots, cut into strips

2 cloves of garlic, cut into strips

grated peel of 1 organic lemon

½ cup (⅛ l) white wine

juice from 1 lemon

2 tablespoons honey

1 cup (¼ l) Chicken Stock (page 46) or canned chicken broth

12 black olives

1 lemon

1 tablespoon cornstarch

1. Preheat the oven to 350°F (177°C). Wash the chickens, pat them dry, and season with salt and pepper, inside and out. Place 2 rosemary leaves inside each chicken.

2. Roast the chickens, breast side up, in the oven for 30 minutes, uncovered. Then turn them breast side down and roast for another 15 minutes.

3. When the chickens have cooked for 10 minutes, add the sliced garlic and shallots to the roasting pan. Add the lemon peel and stir in the white wine.

4. After the chicken has cooked for 30 minutes, mix the lemon juice with the honey and generously brush the mixture all over the outside of the chicken. Baste the chickens several times while they

cook. If the juices in the roasting pan begin to dry out, add some chicken stock.

5. Halve the olives and take out the pits.

6. When the chickens are done, transfer them to a covered baking dish and keep them warm in the turned off oven.

7. Place the roasting pan on the stove, add the rest of the chicken stock, and bring the sauce to a boil over moderate heat. Add the olives and let the sauce boil gently for a few minutes.

8. Peel the lemons well. Cut out the segments (see page 23) and add them to the sauce. Thicken the sauce with cornstarch dissolved in a little bit of cold water. Divide the chicken into pieces and serve with the sauce.

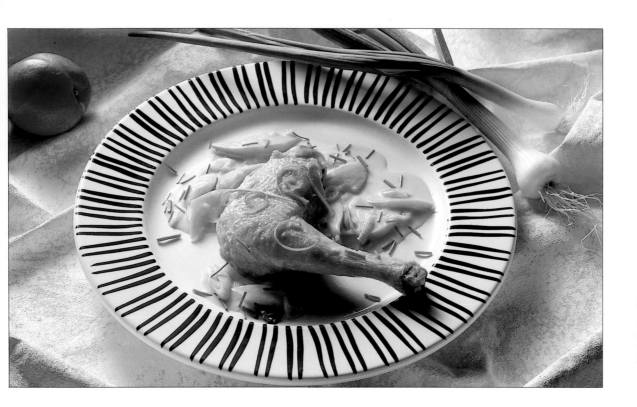

Chicken with Nectarines and Scallions

This delicious dish is so easy to prepare that it just might become a family favorite.

Makes 4 servings

2 whole chickens, 1¾ to 2 pounds (800 g) each

salt and white pepper to taste

1 tablespoon sweet butter

2 nectarines

2 scallions, cut into thin rings

2 shallots, minced

juice and zested skin of 1 lime

¾ cup (200 ml) Chicken Stock (page 46) or canned chicken broth

⅔ cup (150 g) sour cream

1 tablespoon chopped chives

1. Wash the chickens thoroughly and pat them dry. Cut them in half with a pair of poultry shears along the spine and breastbone. Separate each half between the breast and the drumstick so that you have 8 pieces altogether.

2. Season the chicken pieces with salt and pepper. Heat the butter in a large skillet. Brown the chicken pieces on the skin side and then turn them over. Cover the skillet with a lid and cook the chicken over low heat for about 15 minutes. If necessary, pour some chicken stock in so that the roast sediment doesn't burn.

3. Meanwhile, wash the nectarines, halve them, take out the stones, and cut the fruit into slices.

4. Remove the chicken pieces from the skillet and keep them warm. Sauté the scallions and shallots in the skillet. Add the nectarines and the lime skin and stir everything well. Pour in the lime juice and the chicken stock.

5. Bring the liquid to a boil and return the chicken to the skillet. Simmer over low heat for 20 to 25 minutes. Finally, stir in the sour cream: do not let the sauce boil. Sprinkle the chives over everything. Serve the chicken with noodles or rice.

Chicken with Kumquats

The pairing of fresh tarragon with sweet kumquats transforms modest chicken into sheer elegance.

‿

Makes 4 servings

4 chicken leg/thigh pieces, 9 ounces (250 g) each
salt and white pepper to taste
3 tablespoons all-purpose flour
4 tablespoons vegetable oil
½ cup (⅛ l) dry white wine
1 cup (¼ l) Chicken Stock (page 46) or canned chicken broth
1 sprig of fresh tarragon
5 or 6 medium kumquats
⅓ cup (100 g) heavy cream

‿

1. Wash the chicken pieces, pat dry, and separate them at the joint with a sharp knife.
2. Season with salt and pepper, and lightly coat with flour.
3. Heat up the oil in a large skillet and brown the chicken. Add the white wine and the chicken stock.
4. Wash the tarragon and pick off the leaves. Set the leaves aside and add the stems to the chicken. Cover the skillet and cook the chicken over low heat for 45 minutes.
5. Wash the kumquats, halve them crosswise, and remove the pits (see page 31). After the chicken has cooked for 25 minutes, add the fruit.
6. When the chicken is done, remove the tarragon stems and transfer to a platter. Add the heavy cream to the sauce cook until creamy. Add the tarragon leaves, and reheat the chicken in the sauce.

Beef Tenderloin with Papaya and Ginger

Instead of beef, you can use duck, chicken, or turkey breast and create an equally sublime dish.

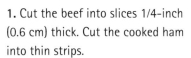

Makes 4 servings

1½ pounds (600 g) beef tenderloin
4 ounces (120 g) cooked ham
2 shallots, minced
1 clove of garlic, minced
large piece of fresh ginger, peeled and cut into fine strips
1 papaya
2 tablespoons sweet butter
salt and freshly ground white pepper to taste
pinch of sweet paprika
1 tablespoon finely chopped parsley
¾ cup (200 ml) Beef Stock (page 46) or canned beef broth
¾ cup (200 g) heavy cream

1. Cut the beef into slices 1/4-inch (0.6 cm) thick. Cut the cooked ham into thin strips.
2. Peel the papaya, remove the pits, and cut into thin slices (see page 32).
3. Melt the butter in a large skillet. Briefly sauté the beef slices on all sides and season with salt and pepper. Remove the beef slices and keep warm in a covered dish.
4. Sauté the shallots and the garlic in the beef juices until transparent. Add the ginger and sauté briefly.
5. Sauté the ham and the papaya and add the paprika and parsley.
6. Pour the beef stock over everything and stir well. Add the heavy cream and let the mixture cook over moderate heat until the sauce thickens.
7. Add the sliced beef. Lower the heat and simmer for 5 minutes. Serve the dish with wide noodles, potatoes or rice.

Sirloin Steak with Spicy Mango Chutney

Spicy chutneys such as the two presented on these pages, greatly enhance the taste of grilled meat, especially when the meat has been marinated.

❧

Marinating time: 1 day
Makes 4 servings

4 sirloin steaks, 5 to 6 ounces (160-180 g) each
1 clove of garlic, finely chopped
1 hot chili pepper, seeded and chopped
1 stem of fresh rosemary
10 to 12 black peppercorns
grated skin of ½ organic lemon
1 cup (¼ l) vegetable oil
salt to taste

FOR THE CHUTNEY
large piece of fresh ginger
1 ½ cups (125 g) red currants
2 ½ cups (500 g) granulated sugar
½ cup (100 ml) wine vinegar
¾ teaspoon cayenne pepper
½ teaspoon salt
2 small green (unripe) mangos

❧

1. One day before serving this dish, place the steaks in a deep dish.
2. Crush the peppercorns with a mortar in a pestle. Wash the rosemary and pick off the leaves. Mix together the pepper, cloves, chili pepper, rosemary, lemon peel, and oil. Pour the marinade over the steaks, cover with plastic wrap, and marinate for 1 day in the refrigerator.

3. Make the chutney 1 day ahead, too. Peel the ginger and finely grate half the piece; finely slice the other half. Crush the red currants with a mortar in a pestle.
4. Cook all the ingredients for the chutney, except the mangos, in a pot over low heat for 15 minutes.
5. In the meantime, peel the mangos, cut the pulp off the stone, and slice it (see page 26). Add the slices to the chutney in the pot and let everything simmer for another 30 minutes over low heat or until the mangos are soft and the chutney has become fairly thick.
6. Pour the hot chutney into sterile glass containers and seal them. Unopened, the chutney will last about six months.
7. On the day you serve this dish, take the steaks out of the marinade and let the oil drain off. Season the meat with salt and grill both sides for a couple of minutes. Serve the steaks with the chutney.

Quince Chutney with Pink Grapefruits

Makes 4 cups (1.2 l) of chutney
6 or 7 medium quinces
4 large shallots, cut into 8 pieces
2 cloves of garlic, finely chopped
3 pink grapefruits
large piece of fresh ginger, peeled and finely sliced
1 teaspoon salt
pinch of pepper
dash of allspice
dash of ground coriander
dash of ground cinnamon
1/4 teaspoon caraway seeds
1 1/2 cups (220 g) light brown sugar
1/2 cup (1/8 l) wine vinegar

1. Peel the quinces, cut them into quarters, cut out the cores, and cut the fruit into small cubes. Combine the quinces, shallots, and garlic in a pot.
2. Squeeze 1 grapefruit into the pot. Carefully peel the other 2 and cut out the segments. Cut the segments into cubes and put them in the pot.
3. Add the sliced ginger, spices, sugar, and vinegar to the quinces, and mix everything well. Bring the mixture to a boil over low heat and let simmer for about 2 hours, stirring frequently. If necessary, skim off the foam.
4. Pour the hot chutney into sterile glass containers and seal.
Unopened, the chutney will last for about 6 months.

Veal in Lemon Mangosteen Sauce

The delicate sweet and sour fruit sauce makes this dish quite distinctive.

Makes 4 servings

2 to 2 ¼ pounds (1 kg) veal shoulder
4 cups (1 l) Beef Stock (page 46) or canned beef broth
1 bunch of soup vegetables consisting of carrots, leeks, and celery, coarsely chopped
1 onion, peeled and coarsely chopped
2 whole cloves
1 bay leaf
salt to taste
2 tablespoons sweet butter
3 tablespoons all-purpose flour
½ cup (100 ml) dry white wine
juice from ½ lemon
1 lemon
5 mangosteens
⅔ cup (150 g) heavy cream
1 egg yolk
1 tablespoon chopped parsley

1. Cut the veal into cubes, 1¼ inch (3 cm) in size, and blanch in hot water. Pour the beef stock into a large pot. Place the veal cubes into the cold stock and bring to a boil. Skim off the foam.
2. Add all the vegetables, the cloves, and the bay leaf to the broth. Season with salt and let the meat cook without the lid for 40 to 55 minutes or until done. Then, take the meat cubes out of the broth and pass the broth through a strainer.
3. Melt the butter in a pot and stir in the flour until it turns pale gold.

Pour in the white wine, stirring constantly. Gradually pour in the meat broth and stir everything until smooth. Season with lemon juice and simmer the sauce for 10 to 15 minutes.
4. In the meantime, peel the lemon, cut out the segments (see page 23), and set aside. Cut open the skins of the mangosteens and divide the fruit into segments (see page 27). Set the fruits aside.
5. Whisk the heavy cream with the egg yolk, pour it into the simmering sauce, and reheat the sauce over moderate heat—do not let it boil. Heat the meat and the fruits in the sauce. Garnish with parsley. Serve with noodeles or potatoes.

Veal Piccata in Mushroom Ragout with Nectarines

This creamy, mellow version of the popular entrée is certain to be well-received.

Makes: 4 servings
FOR THE PICCATA
1¾ pounds (800 g) veal breast
1 small onion, cut in quarters
2 whole cloves
1 bay leaf
½ cups (⅛ l) dry white wine
salt to taste
2 tablespoons all-purpose flour
2 eggs
2 tablespoons grated Parmesan cheese
1 tablespoon sweet butter

FOR THE MUSHROOM RAGOUT
1 pound (500 g) mushrooms, several varieties, washed and sliced
1 shallot, minced
1 tablespoon sweet butter
salt and pepper to taste
½ cup (⅛ l) dry white wine
½ cup (125 g) heavy cream
2 nectarines

1. Put the breast of veal, onion quarters, cloves, bay leaf, and white wine into a large pot and fill with water so that the veal is covered with plenty of water. Bring the liquid to a boil over moderate heat. Skim off the foam, add salt, and simmer the veal over low heat for 15 minutes. Then, remove the pot from the stove and let the veal cool off in the broth.
2. Melt the butter in a skillet and sauté the shallots until transparent, then add the mushrooms and sauté lightly. Season with salt and pepper.
3. Pour in the white wine and let the sauce thicken over low heat. Add the heavy cream and cook the mushroom ragout until the sauce reduces and is creamy.
4. Wash the nectarines, halve them, and remove the stones. Cut the halves into thin slices and add them to the mushroom ragout.
5. Take the veal out of the broth, dab it dry, and cut into 1-inch (2.54 cm) pieces. Season with salt and pepper and coat with flour.
6. In a bowl, whisk the eggs and stir in the Parmesan cheese. Coat the veal with this mixture. Melt the butter in a large skillet and brown the veal over moderate heat until golden brown. Serve the veal with the mushroom ragout.

Ham Ragout with Pineapple

For a fancy appetizer or a special snack, serve this delicious ragout in small puff pastry shells.

❧

Makes 4 servings

FOR THE HAM

2 to 2 ¼ pounds (1 kg) cooked ham

1½ cups (400 ml) Beef Stock (page 46) or canned beef broth

3 shallots, finely chopped

2 tablespoons sweet butter (divided)

1 teaspoon curry powder

1 tablespoon all-purpose flour

⅓ cup (100 g) heavy cream

2 baby pineapples or 1 small pineapple

salt and freshly ground white pepper to taste

❧

1. Cut the ham into bite-size cubes.

2. Melt 1 tablespoon of butter in a skillet and sauté the shallots until transparent. Sprinkle the curry powder and flour over the shallots and sauté for another 2 minutes.

3. Slowly pour the beef stock in with the shallots and stir. Simmer the sauce over low heat for 6 to 8 minutes. Add the heavy cream and let everything reduce for 5 minutes. Break the remaining tablespoon of cold butter into little flakes and whisk into the simmering sauce.

4. Peel the baby pineapples, cut them into 4 pieces, remove the fruit from the stalks, and cut them into small cubes (see page 37). Add the pineapple and the ham cubes to the sauce and simmer for 5 minutes. Season with salt and pepper. Serve the ragout with rice or noodles.

Pork Steak with Hazelnut Crust and Tamarillo Sauce

The fruit sauce and the nutty crust are a great pairing of tastes.

❧

Makes 4 servings

FOR THE SAUCE

4 tamarillos
2 shallots, finely chopped
1 tablespoon sweet butter
salt and white pepper to taste
4 tablespoons port
1 cup (250 ml) Beef Stock (page 46) or canned beef broth
1 teaspoon cornstarch

FOR THE MEAT

3 ½ ounces (100 g) ground hazelnuts
1¼ cups (120 g) bread crumbs
4 boneless pork steaks, 4 ½ ounces (130 g) each
salt and white pepper to taste
4 tablespoons all-purpose flour
1 egg
6 tablespoons vegetable oil
1 tablespoon sweet butter
some lemon juice

❧

1. Peel the tamarillos (see page 44). Cut 1 tamarillo into thin slices and set aside. Cut the 3 others into cubes.

2. Melt the butter in a skillet and sauté the shallots until transparent. Add the tamarillo cubes and sauté for 2 minutes. Season with salt and pepper. Add the port and the beef stock and simmer for 5 minutes.

3. In a bowl, mix the hazelnuts and the bread crumbs. Season the pork with salt and pepper and dredge them in the flour. Whisk the egg in a bowl and coat the pork first with egg and then with the hazelnut–bread crumb mixture. Slightly press the coating on.

4. When the tamarillo sauce has reduced and thickened, purée it until it is thoroughly blended. Pour the sauce back into the pot and reheat. If necessary, thicken with cornstarch that has been dissolved in a small amount of cold water.

5. Heat the oil in a large skillet and cook each side of the pork steaks for 5 minutes over moderate heat; the hazelnut–bread crumb coating should be crispy.

6. Add the sliced tamarillos and briefly sauté them. Sprinkle some lemon juice over the steaks.

7. Remove the pork from the skillet and drain on paper towels. Serve with the sauce and the tamarillo slices. Rice or potatoes are a nice complement to this dish.

Pork Chops in Plum Sauce

The flavor and aroma of this plum sauce add zest to broiled pork.

Makes 4 servings

4 center-cut pork chops, 7 ounces (200 g) each

white pepper

FOR THE SAUCE

3 medium plums

1 tablespoon sweet butter

salt and white pepper to taste

½ cup (⅛ l) Beef Stock (page 46) or canned beef broth

dash of powdered ginger

¼ cinnamon stick

1 whole clove

splash of balsamic vinegar

1 teaspoon sweet butter, chilled and cut into cubes

1. Season the pork chops with pepper. Place them on a broiling pan and broil in the oven, turning the chops once. When the meat is cooked, keep them warm in a covered dish.
2. Wash the plums, halve them, and remove the stones (see page 38).
3. Melt the butter in a skillet. Add the plum halves and season with salt and pepper. Pour in the beef stock. Add the ginger, cinnamon, and clove, and simmer the sauce over low heat for 5 to 7 minutes or until the plums fall apart and the sauce is slightly thick.
4. Season the sauce with balsamic vinegar. Remove the cinnamon stick and the cloves and stir the cold butter cubes into the simmering sauce.
5. Serve the pork chops on top of the plum sauce. As a side dish, mashed or fried potatoes go well.

Lamb Shanks in Cranberry Red Wine Sauce

This hearty entrée is sure to warm the spirits of family and friends.

Marinating time: 24 hours
Makes 4 servings

4 lamb shanks, 8½ to 10½ ounces (250 to 300 g) each

2 medium onions, finely sliced

2 cloves of garlic, minced

1 large carrot, sliced

1 bay leaf

2 stems of fresh thyme

2 stems of fresh rosemary

8 to 10 peppercorns

3 to 4 whole allspice

2 whole cloves

salt and pepper to taste

3 cups (¾ l) hearty red wine

4 tablespoons oil

1 tablespoon tomato paste

1½ cups (150 g) cranberries

1. Put the lamb shanks in a large bowl. Add the garlic, onion, and carrot. Slightly crush the fresh herbs and whole spices in a pestle with a mortar and add, too. Pour the red wine over the meat, cover the bowl, and let the lamb marinate for 24 hours in the refrigerator.
2. The next day, take the shanks out of the marinade and let them drain on a paper towel. Pour the marinade through a strainer into a large pot, bring to a boil, and remove the foam. Set the vegetables aside in the strainer.
3. Preheat the oven to 350°F (177°C). Heat the oil in a large skillet and brown the shanks evenly on all sides. Add the marinated vegetables and sauté them until slightly brown.
4. Stir in the tomato paste and continue to cook everything for 5 minutes. Pour in all of the marinade and bring to a boil. Wash the cranberries and add them.
5. Transfer the lamb to a large baking dish and roast in the oven, covered, for 1 to 1½ hours. The shanks are done when you can easily stick a fork into the muscular leg meat. Keep them warm in the turned-off oven.
6. Pour the sauce through a strainer into a pot. Use the back of a spoon to push the vegetables and the cranberries through the strainer. Reheat the shanks in the sauce and season with salt and pepper. Serve with dumplings or polenta.

Lamb Medallions with Seville Orange Sauce

A generous serving of tangy orange sauce tastes superb with these succulent medallions.

Makes 4 servings

1½ pounds (600 g) boneless lamb, cut into 12 slices and pounded to ⅛-inch (3 mm) thickness

pepper to taste

12 fresh sage leaves

6 thin slices of prosciutto

3 tablespoons vegetable oil

1 tablespoon sweet butter

FOR THE SAUCE

1 to 2 Seville oranges (bitter)

½ clove of garlic, finely minced

¾ cup (200 ml) Beef Stock (page 46) or canned beef broth

½ tablespoon honey

1 teaspoon cornstarch

salt and white pepper to taste

1. Season the lamb medallions with pepper and place 1 sage leaf on each one.

2. Halve the proscuitto lengthwise and wrap each medallion in 1 slice. If necessary, fasten with toothpicks.

3. Heat the oil in a large skillet until very hot and carefully sauté the medallions for 3 minutes. Then turn them over and sauté another 3 minutes. Add the butter and cook the lamb for 2 minutes.

4. In the meantime, squeeze the Seville oranges. If these are unavailable, use the juice from 1 large orange.

5. Take the medallions out of the skillet and keep warm in a covered dish.

6. Briefly sauté the garlic in the roast sediment. Add the orange juice and let the liquid reduce by half over low heat. Pour in the beef stock and stir in the honey. Cook the sauce for several minutes, then thicken with cornstarch dissolved in a little bit of cold water. Serve the lamb medallions with the sauce and angel hair pasta.

Lamb Curry in Lemon Sauce

Lemons add distinction and zing to an easy-to-prepare curried dish.

∼

Makes 4 servings

1¾ pounds (800 g) lamb shoulder with bones removed

2 medium onions, cut into rings

2 tablespoons sweet butter

1 hot green chili, seeded and chopped

salt to taste

2 tablespoons curry powder

juice from 2 lemons

2 organic lemons

∼

1. Cut the lamb into cubes, about 1¼ inches (3 cm) in size.

2. Melt the butter in a large pot and sauté the onions until golden. Add the chili and sauté for 1 minute.

3. Salt the lamb and add it to the onions. Sprinkle in the curry powder and pour in the lemon juice. Cover the pot with a lid.

4. Simmer the lamb over low heat for about 1 hour. If the juices cook out, add some water.

5. With a zester, thinly peel the skin of half a lemon, chop it finely, and add to the lamb curry. Peel all the lemons and cut out the segments (see page 23). When the lamb is cooked, add the lemon segments, cook for 2 minutes, and serve with rice or couscous.

Turkey Kabobs with Fruit

You can make these kabobs (also great barbecued) with chicken breast or pork instead of turkey.

⤳

Makes 4 servings

1½ pounds (600 g) turkey tenderloin

4 small chicken livers

4 slices of bacon

8 Cape gooseberries

1⅓ cups (200 g) pineapple without skin

1 sour apple

1 small onion

4 tablespoons vegetable oil

1 tablespoon sweet butter

⤳

1. Cut the turkey into bite-size pieces. Wrap 1 slice of bacon around each chicken liver. Refrigerate the meat.
2. Remove the gooseberries from the calyxes (see page 12) and wash them. Cut the pineapple into 8 pieces. Wash the apple, cut it into 4 pieces, cut out the core, and halve each quarter. Peel the onions and cut them into 4 pieces.
3. Skewer the prepared ingredients onto spits in the following order: apple, turkey, onion, gooseberry, bacon-covered chicken liver, pineapple, apple, turkey, gooseberry, pineapple.
4. Heat the oil in a large skillet until very hot and fry the kabobs until the meat is done, turning them several times during cooking. Remove the spits, let the butter foam up in the roast sediment, and pour it over the meat and fruit. Serve with wild rice and a fresh salad.

Turkey with Fig Beignets

Moist turkey and sweet fig fritters make an unusual and flavorful entrée.

⤳

Makes 4 servings

1½ pounds (600 g) turkey tenderloin

2 slices of bacon

1 small carrot, peeled and chopped

1 stalk of celery, chopped

2 shallots, minced

½ cup chopped leek

salt and pepper to taste

2 tablespoons vegetable oil

½ cup (⅛ l) dry red wine

2 cups (½ l) Chicken Stock (page 46) or canned chicken broth

½ teaspoon cornstarch

FOR THE BEIGNETS

1 cup (125 g) all-purpose flour

½ cup (⅛ l) light beer

2 eggs

pinch of salt

4 figs

2 cups (½ l) vegetable oil for frying

⤳

1. Cut the turkey into bite-size pieces. Cut the bacon into fine strips. Preheat the oven to 350°F (177°C).
2. Salt and pepper the turkey pieces. Heat the oil on the stove in an oven-safe pot and brown the turkey. Add the bacon and all the vegetables. Cook for 5 minutes.
3. Quench the vegetables with the wine and chicken stock. Transfer the pot to the oven and cook for 20 minutes.
4. For the beignets, sift the flour into a bowl and stir in the beer.
5. Separate the eggs and blend the yolks into the mix. Whisk the egg whites stiff and blend them into the beer dough.
6. Peel the figs (see page 18), dredge them in flour, and coat them with beer dough. Heat the vegetable oil in a deep fat fryer or deep pot until very hot and fry the beignets golden brown. Drain them on paper towels.
7. Remove the turkey from the pot and keep the meat warm in a covered dish. Put the pot back on the stove and cook down the sauce to half the amount. Mix the cornstarch with a little bit of cold water, thicken the sauce as needed, and season with salt and pepper.
8. Serve the turkey with the sauce and the fig beignets, cut into halves. Little potato dumplings or potatoes complement this dish.

Seafood

The texture and aroma of fresh seafood are
tastefully complemented by fruit. Combining
seafood and fruits offers cooks a wide range of
delicious and attractive looking dishes.

Salmon Fillets with Cold Avocado and Watercress Sauce

The combination of salmon, vegetables, and fruit makes this a delightful summer meal.

Makes 4 servings

4 salmon fillets, skin on, 5 ounces (140 g) each
some lemon juice
4 or 5 small potatoes, peeled and finely sliced
1 large zucchini, peeled and finely sliced
3 tablespoons sweet butter (divided)
salt and white pepper to taste
½ clove of garlic, minced

FOR THE SAUCE
1 ripe avocado
juice from ½ lemon
½ cup (100 g) sour cream
salt and white pepper to taste
some drops Worcestershire sauce
1 bunch of watercress

1. Wash the fish and pat dry. Trickle lemon juice onto the fillets and refrigerate them.
2. Place the potato slices in cold water and soak them for 10 minutes or until the starch comes out. Drain and pat dry.
3. Heat 1 tablespoon of butter in a skillet and fry the potatoes over moderate heat for about 10 minutes, turning them frequently.
4. For the sauce, peel the avocado, halve it, remove the stone, and scoop out the pulp with a spoon (see page 9). Cut half into small cubes and trickle lemon juice over them.
5. Puree the other half of the avocado in a blender. Spoon it into a bowl and mix in the sour cream. Season with pepper and Worcestershire sauce.
6. Wash the watercress, pat dry, and cut the leaves off the stems. Set some leaves aside for garnishing and chop the remaining ones finely. Stir the chopped watercress and the avocado cubes into the sauce.
7. Season the fried potato slices with salt and pepper and transfer them to a covered dish to keep warm.
8. Clean the skillet with paper towels. Melt 1 tablespoon of butter. Season the fillets with salt and pepper and fry them on the skin side in the hot butter until the skin turns crispy. Turn them over and fry the other side for 3 or 4 minutes. Remove the fish and keep it warm, covered.
9. Heat the remaining tablespoon of butter in the pan. Sauté the minced garlic. Add the zucchini slices and fry them on both sides until golden brown.
10. Arrange the potato and zucchini slices on plates and place the salmon fillets on them. Garnish the avocado sauce with the remaining watercress and serve it with the fish.

Bacon-Seasoned Pike with Banana-Peanut Butter Sauce

This entrée is rich and distinctive. It works well with salmon, sole, or red snapper.

Makes 4 servings

4 pike fillets, 6 ounces (180 g) each
2 slices streaky bacon
4 or 5 medium potatoes
1 banana
2 tablespoons lemon juice
2 tablespoons curry powder
4 tablespoons plain yogurt

salt and cayenne pepper to taste
2 tablespoons salted peanuts
2 tablespoons vegetable oil
white pepper to taste
1 tablespoon sweet butter
1 tablespoon chopped parsley

1. Wash the fish fillets and pat dry. Cut the bacon into fine strips and loosely insert them into each fillet on one side. To do so, use a sharp knife to cut small pockets in the fish and slip in the bacon strips. Cover and refrigerate the fish.

2. Peel the potatoes, wash them, and cut them lengthwise into 4 strips. Cook the potatoes in salted water for about 20 minutes.

3. In the meantime, peel the banana, cut it into slices, and finely puree it in a food processor with the lemon juice and curry powder. Put the mixture in a bowl, stir in the yogurt, and season well with salt and cayenne pepper.

4. Finely chop the peanuts and blend them into the sauce.

5. Heat the oil in the pan. Season the fish with pepper and cook them on the side with the bacon strips. Cook for 3 to 4 minutes, then turn them over, and cook the other side for 3 to 4 minutes. Finally, add the butter and the parsley and cook for 1 minute. Put the fillets onto plates and pour the parsley butter over them.

6. Drain the potatoes and distribute them onto the plates, along with the sauce.

Pike with Lime-Fennel Sauce and Star Fruit

The interplay of fennel, lime, and star fruit makes this dish visually intriguing and quite delicious.

Makes 4 servings

FOR THE SAUCE
2 fennel bulbs
1 shallot, cut into thin rings
1 tablespoon sweet butter
salt and white pepper to taste
2 limes
1½ cups (400 ml) Fish Stock (page 47)
¾ cup (200 g) heavy cream

FOR THE FISH
2 tomatoes
4 pike fillets, 6 ounces (180 g) each, skinless
salt and white pepper to taste
3 tablespoons vegetable oil
1 star fruit

1. Cut the greens off the fennel bulbs and set them aside. Halve the bulbs, cut out the stalks, and cut the vegetables into fine slices.
2. Melt the butter in a skillet and sauté the shallots until transparent. Add the fennel, season with salt and pepper, and sauté for 3 to 4 minutes.
3. Grate the lime peel and squeeze the juice. Add the juice and the peel to the sauce, pour in the fish stock, and let the sauce simmer over low heat, covered, for 20 to 25 minutes.
4. Cut the tomatoes crosswise and remove the skin. Halve them, remove the seeds, and cut out the stem. Cut the tomato into cubes.
5. Wash the fillets and pat dry.
6. Heat the oil in a large skillet and cook the pike fillets on both sides for 3 to 4 minutes. The fish is done when you can easily poke through the fillet with a knife tip.
7. Wash the star fruit, round the edges (see page 42), and slice the fruit.
8. Remove the fish from the skillet and keep it warm, covered. Clean the skillet with paper towels. Warm the star fruit slices in the skillet. Add the tomato cubes and let everything cook over low heat for 5 to 7 minutes.
9. Now add the heavy cream to the lime-fennel sauce and let it cook until it becomes creamy. Wash the fennel greens, chop them finely, and add them to the sauce.
10. Peel the second lime, cut out the segments (see page 23) and briefly warm them in the lime-fennel sauce. Season the sauce with salt and pepper.
11. Distribute the sauce onto the plates, serve the pike fillets on top, and add the star fruit–tomato ragout. Mashed potatoes complement this dish well.

Variation: You can substitute red snapper, sole, or salmon.

Flounder and Salmon Roulade with Cherimoya Sauce

Here's an unusual way to prepare fish, delicately flavored with a mild fruit sauce.

Makes 4 servings
1 pound (454 g) flounder, bones and skin removed
salt and white pepper to taste

²/₃ cup (150 g) heavy cream, chilled
4 slices of salmon, 5 to 6 ounces (160 g) each, cut from the middle of a large salmon fillet

FOR THE SAUCE
1 cherimoya
2 shallots, minced
1 tablespoon sweet butter
salt and white pepper to taste
4 to 5 saffron threads
1¼ cups (300 g) heavy cream, chilled
some lemon juice

1. Cut the flounder into small cubes and put them in the freezer for 10 minutes. Season with salt and pepper and puree the flounder in a food processor. Add the cold heavy cream little by little, until it's well blended. Refrigerate the purée for 10 minutes and then use the back of a spoon to push it through a fine strainer.

2. Cut the salmon slices horizontally; don't cut through all the way.

Fold the fillets apart and beat slightly flat.

3. Spread the flounder purée on the salmon slices. Roll up the salmon slices and wrap them in cheesecloth. Twist the ends of the cloth to make knots. Refrigerate the fish rolls for 15 minutes.

4. Peel the cherimoya, cut it in half, and remove the pits (see page 13). Push the fruit through a strainer.

5. Melt the butter in a pot and sauté the shallots until transparent. Add the cherimoya purée and season with salt and pepper. Cook over moderate heat for 5 minutes and then pour in the heavy cream, stirring frequently. Cook over low heat until the sauce becomes creamy, then pass it through a strainer and stir in the lemon juice.

6. Fill a pot with a few inches of water and bring the water to a boil over moderate heat. Lower the heat to simmer and immerse the wrapped fish rolls. If the water does not cover the fish by 1 inch (2.54 cm), add more water. When the water begins to simmer again, cover the pot and begin timing. Poach the fish for 15 to 20 minutes. Never let the water boil.

7. Remove the rolls from the pot and carefully take off the wrapping. Slice the rolls and serve them with the sauce. Wild rice goes very well with these roulades.

Cod with Horseradish Crust and Cactus Pear Sauce

Both sweet and tangy, this fish goes well with steamed broccoli and boiled red potatoes.

❧

Makes 4 servings

4 cactus pears

3 tablespoons sweet butter, chilled (divided)

1 tablespoon granulated sugar

4 tablespoons red port

1/2 cup (1/8 l) Chicken Stock (page 46) or canned chicken broth

salt and white pepper to taste

2 tablespoons freshly ground horseradish

2 slices of toast

4 pieces of cod, 5 ounces (140 g) each

3 tablespoons vegetable oil

some fresh basil leaves, finely chopped

❧

1. Peel the cactus pears (see page 11) and slice them with a knife.
2. Melt 1 tablespoon of butter in a pot. Add the sugar and let it caramelize slightly. Add the cactus pear slices and sauté them for 5 minutes.
3. Add the port and the chicken stock. Simmer over low heat until the fruits fall apart and the stock reduces to half the amount. Use the back of a spoon to push the sauce through a strainer, and season with salt and pepper.
4. Stir 1 tablespoon of butter in a bowl until it is soft. Blend in the horseradish. Cut the crusts off the toast and grind them up coarsely in a food processor. Stir the bread-crumbs into the butter-horseradish mix. Transfer it to a plate and refrigerate it for 10 minutes.
5. Spread the horseradish mixture onto each fillet. Bake the fish at 300°F (148.8°C) for 7 to 10 minutes, or until the fish flakes easily and the crust turns golden brown.
6. Reheat the cactus pears. Crumble the remaining tablespoon of butter into little flakes and stir it into the simmering sauce. Add the basil and season with salt and pepper. Serve the sauce with the fish.

Monkfish with Sliced Persimmon and Curry Sauce

Curry and yogurt nicely complement the fruits and seafood in this light dish.

❧

Makes 4 servings

FOR THE CURRY SAUCE

1 tart apple

1/2 banana

2 shallots, minced

1 tablespoon sweet butter

1 tablespoon curry powder

1 teaspoon all-purpose flour

1/2 cup (1/8 l) dry white wine

2 cups (1/2 l) Fish Stock (page 47)

salt and pepper to taste

2 tablespoons plain yogurt

IN ADDITION

1 pound (454 g) monkfish

salt and white pepper to taste

4 tablespoons all-purpose flour

6 tablespoons vegetable oil

1 1/2 tablespoons butter

2 persimmons

❧

1. Peel the apple, cut it into 4 pieces, and cut out the core. Cut the quarters into small slices. Peel the banana and slice it.
2. Melt the butter in a pot and sauté the shallots until transparent. Add the apple and banana slices and cook them for 2 to 3 minutes. Sprinkle the curry powder over everything, add the flour, and stir well. Pour in the white wine and stir the sauce until smooth. Add the fish stock and let the sauce simmer for 15 to 20 minutes.
3. Skin off the monkfish's purplish outer membrane and cut the fish into 2-inch (5.1 cm) pieces. Season with salt and white pepper. Lightly coat the fish in 2 tablespoons of flour and tap off the extra flour.
4. Heat the oil in a skillet and cook the fish over low heat for 3 to 4 minutes on each side. Add 1/2 tablespoon of butter to the skillet and cook another 2 minutes. Set the fish aside in a covered dish.
5. Peel the persimmons, slice them (see page 36), and coat them in what remains of the flour. Wipe out the skillet with paper towels. Melt the remaining tablespoon of butter and cook the persimmons for 2 to 3 minutes.
6. Puree the curry sauce in a food processor and stir in the yogurt.
7. Arrange the persimmon slices on a plate, place the monkfish on top, and pour the curry sauce over everything. Cooked rice goes well with this dish.

Cod with Pineapple

The mild flavor of the fish is nicely accented by the tanginess of pineapple in this easy-to-prepare entrée.

Makes 4 servings

1 1/2 pounds (600 g) cod
2 shallots, minced
1 tablespoon sweet butter (divided)
salt and white pepper to taste
juice from 1/2 lemon
1 cup (1/4 l) Fish Stock (page 47)
1 baby pineapple
2 tablespoons all-purpose flour
1/2 teaspoon curry powder
1/3 cup (100 g) heavy cream

1. Cut the cod into 4 pieces of equal size.

2. Place the shallots in a skillet. Season the fish pieces with salt, pepper, and lemon juice, and place them on top of the shallots. Pour in the fish stock. Heat the liquid over moderate heat, but do not let it boil. Simmer the fish over low heat for 5 to 7 minutes or until the fish flakes easily.

3. In the meantime, peel the baby pineapple (see page 37), remove the stalk with an apple corer, and cut the fruit into 8 slices.

4. Melt 1/2 tablespoon of butter in a pan. Coat the pineapple slices in flour and cook them in the butter until they are golden brown.

5. Transfer the fish to a covered dish to keep warm. Remove the pineapple slices from the pan and keep them warm, also.

6. Cook the sauce until it reduces by half. Knead the curry powder with the rest of the butter and refrigerate it for 5 minutes. Pour the sauce through a fine strainer into another pot and add the heavy cream. Bring the sauce to a boil, add the curried butter, and stir well.

7. Serve the cod with the pineapple slices and pour the curry sauce over everything. Serve with rice cooked with fresh or canned tomatoes.

Mussel Ragout with Lychees and Pink Grapefruit

This dish is easy to prepare and sure to please. Serve it with fresh French bread and dry white wine.

❧

Makes 4 servings

6 to 7 pounds (3 kg) mussels
2 shallots, minced
1 clove of garlic, minced
1 carrot, diced
1 celery stalk, diced
1 pink grapefruit
16 lychees
4 tablespoons olive oil
2 cups (400 ml) dry white wine
1 tablespoon finely cut peppermint

❧

1. Thoroughly clean the mussels under cold running water. Throw out any mussels that are already open. On the remaining ones, cut off the rough beard with a knife.
2. Peel the grapefruit, cut out the segments (see page 21), and squeeze the juice from the fruit walls into a bowl. Peel the lychees, halve them, and remove the pits (see page 25).

3. Heat the olive oil in a large pot and sauté the shallots and the garlic until glassy. Briefly sauté the vegetables as well.
4. Add the mussels and pour in the white wine. Cover the pot and cook the mussels over moderate heat for 8 to 10 minutes, until all the shells have opened.

5. After about 7 minutes, add the grapefruit juice and segments, and the lychees. Pick out any unopened mussels and throw them away. Serve the mussel ragout in deep plates and garnish with peppermint.

Red Snapper with Fried Guavas and Curried Risotto

The unusual tastes and texture of crispy sesame crust, fried fruit, and cheesy, curried rice make this an exotic and delicious dish.

Makes 4 servings

FOR THE RISOTTO

1 shallot, minced

½ clove of garlic, minced

1 cup (200 g) risotto rice

2 tablespoons sweet butter (divided)

1 teaspoon curry powder

½ cup (⅛ l) dry white wine

2 cups (½ l) Fish Stock (page 47)

2 tablespoons finely grated Parmesan cheese

IN ADDITION

4 red snapper fillets, 4 ounces (120 g) each, skin removed

2 guavas

2 tablespoons sesame seeds

6 tablespoons vegetable oil

1 tablespoon sweet butter

salt and white pepper to taste

2 tablespoons all-purpose flour

1. Wash the risotto and let it drain.
2. Melt 2 tablespoons of butter in a pot and sauté the shallots and the garlic for 3 to 4 minutes. Add the risotto and sauté until it becomes glassy, stirring constantly. Stir in the curry powder and then add the white wine. Simmer the risotta, uncovered, over low heat for about 15 minutes. Then add a little fish stock and stir the risotta well. Continue to cook and stir until the risotta is tender, always adding more fish stock to keep the risotta slightly covered with liquid.
3. Wash the fillets and pat dry. Peel the guaves and slice them (see page 21).
4. When the risotta is done, remove the pot from the stove.
5. Put the sesame seeds on a plate. Season the snapper fillets with salt and pepper and press them, skin side down, onto the sesame seeds.
6. Heat the oil in skillet and sauté the fillets on the skin side for about 3 minutes until they are crisp. (Be careful not to get the oil too hot or the sesame seeds will burn.) Turn the fillets over and sauté the other side for 3 minutes. Transfer the fillets to a covered dish to keep them warm.
7. Wipe the skillet with paper towels and melt the butter in it. Season the guavas with salt and pepper, dredge them in flour, and fry them on both sides until golden brown.
8. Blend the Parmesan cheese and the remaining ½ tablespoon of butter into the risotto. If necessary, add a little more fish stock. Serve the risotto with the red snapper and sliced guava.

juice from $1/2$ lemon
salt and white pepper to taste
2 tablespoons all-purpose flour
4 tablespoons olive oil

1. For the fritter dough, sift the flour into a bowl and stir in the wine. Blend in the egg yolks and salt the batter. Refrigerate the dough for 20 minutes.

2. Melt the butter in a pot and sauté the shallots until transparent. Briefly sauté the ginger. Stir in the honey, the lemon peel, and two-thirds of the lemon juice.

3. Add the fish stock and let the liquid reduce by half over moderate heat. Add the crème fraîche and simmer the sauce over low heat until it becomes creamy.

4. Peel the nashis, halve them, and remove the pits. Cut the nashi halves into bite-size wedges. Dredge them in 2 tablespoons of flour. Whisk the egg whites until stiff and blend them into the fritter dough.

5. Heat the vegetable oil in a deep-fat fryer or deep pot until very hot. Coat the fruit wedges with fritter dough and fry them for 8 to 10 minutes. Drain the fritters on paper towels.

6. Trickle lemon juice on the fish and season with salt and pepper. Lightly coat them in flour. Heat the olive oil in a large skillet and sauté the fillets on the skin side for 2 to 3 minutes. To keep the fish flat and allow the skin to crisp, press down on them with a spatula. Turn the fillets over and sauté the other side for about 2 minutes.

7. Add the peppermin to the sauceand bring to a boil. Serve the red snapper with the nashi fritters and the sauce.

Red Snapper with Nashi Fritters and Ginger Sauce

This novel dish is sweet and piquant and will liven up any kind of mild fish.

Makes 4 servings
FOR THE FRITTERS
1 cup (125 g) all-purpose flour
$1/2$ cup ($1/8$ l) dry white wine
2 egg yolks
pinch of salt
4 ripe nashis (or ripe pears)
2 tablespoons all-purpose flour
2 egg whites

2 cups ($1/2$ l) vegetable oil for deep frying

FOR THE SAUCE
4 shallots, minced
large piece of fresh ginger, peeled and cut into strips
1 tablespoon sweet butter
$1/2$ tablespoon honey
grated skin of $1/2$ organic lemon
juice from 1 lemon
$1/2$ cup ($1/8$ l) Fish Stock (page 47)
$1/2$ tablespoon Crème Fraîche (page 47) or sour cream
fresh peppermint leaves, cut into strips

FOR THE FISH
8 red snapper fillets, 2 to 3 ounces (60 to 80 g) each, skin on

Mahi-Mahi with Tamarillos and Wild Rice

The slightly chewy texture of mahi-mahi and wild rice are nicely complemented by the smooth texture and taste of tamarillos.

❧

Makes 4 servings

3/4 cup (120 g) wild rice
4 tamarillos
4 tablespoons sweet butter (divided)
pinch of granulated sugar
splash of lemon juice
2 tablespoons port
1 cup (1/4 l) Fish Stock (page 47)
salt to taste
dash of cayenne pepper
4 mahi-mahi fillets, 4 to 5 ounces (120 to 150 g) each, skin on
white pepper to taste
2 tablespoons all-purpose flour
5 tablespoons olive oil

❧

1. Wash the rice and let it soak in cold water for 1 to 2 hours. Then let it drain, put it into boiling water, and let it simmer for about 45 minutes. Then pour out the water.
2. In the meantime, peel the tamarillos (see page 44). Cut the fruit into 8 slices, about 1/4 inch (0.6 cm) thick, and cut the remaining fruit pulp into cubes.
3. Melt 1 teaspoon of butter in a pot and sauté the tamarillo cubes. Add sugar, lemon juice, and port and cook everything until the liquid has almost boiled away.
4. Add the fish stock and cook the tamarillo cubes until soft. Then

add 2 teaspoons of butter and puree everything in a food processor. Season the sauce with salt and cayenne pepper.
5. Season the mahi-mahi with salt and pepper and flour lightly.
6. Heat the oil in a skillet and sauté the fillets on the skin side for about 3 minutes. To keep the fillets flat and allow the skin to crisp, press down on them with a spatula. Turn the fillets over and sauté the other side for about 3 minutes. Transfer the fish to a covered dish to keep them warm.
7. Wipe out the skillet with paper towels. Melt the remaining teaspoon of butter and slightly sauté the tamarillo slices that were not yet used. Reheat the sauce. Serve the mahi-mahi fillets with the tamarillo slices, the sauce, and the wild rice.

Halibut Steak in Vegetable Sauce with Fried Fruit

The mild vegetable sauce provides a nice background for the sweet and tart fried fruit.

❧

Makes 4 servings
FOR THE FISH
1 carrot, peeled and diced
2 celery stalks, diced
3/4 cup finely chopped leeks
1 tablespoon sweet butter, chilled
salt and white pepper to taste
1 cup (1/4 l) Fish Stock (page 47)
juice from 1/2 lemon
4 halibut steaks, 7 ounces (200 g) each
fresh tarragon leaves, finely cut

FOR THE FRUITS
1 banana
1 kiwi
1 peach
1 grapefruit
5 tablespoons all-purpose flour
2 eggs
2 cups (200 g) bread crumbs
1/3 cup (100 ml) vegetable oil

❧

1. Melt 1/2 tablespoon butter in a flat casserole and sauté the chopped vegetables. Season with salt and pepper and pour in the fish stock. Add the lemon juice and bring the liquid to a boil. Reduce the heat and cook for 5 minutes.
2. Place the halibut on top of the vegetables. Cover the pot and simmer over low heat for 10 minutes.
3. Peel the banana and cut it crosswise into 1/2-inch-thick (1 cm) slices. Peel the kiwi and cut it into 2-inch-thick (5 cm) slices. Wash the peach, halve it, remove the stone, and cut the fruit with the skin into bite-size pieces. Peel the grapefruit and cut out the segments (see page 21).
4. Place the fruits on paper towels and pat dry. Dredge them in the flour. Whisk the eggs and coat the fruit, first in the egg batter and then in bread crumbs. Press the breading on well.
5. Heat the vegetable oil in a deep skillet and deep-fry the fruits until golden brown. Drain the fruit and keep warm.
6. Remove the halibut steaks from the vegetable mixture and keep warm. Stir in the remaining 1/2 tablespoon of cold butter, add the tarragon, and simmer for 2 minutes. Serve the fish as show in the photo.

Sole with Fruit Sauce

This dish has a fresh, citrus flavor that perfectly suits the mild-tasting fish.

～

Makes 4 servings

8 sole fillets, about 3 ounces (80 g) each
1 carrot, cut into fine strips
2 celery stalks, cut into fine strips
1 tablespoon sweet butter
salt and white pepper to taste
1 cherimoya
2 oranges
1 lime

1 tablespoon pickled red peppercorns
1 stem of fresh lemon balm or peppermint

～

1. Preheat the oven to 425°F (220°C). Wash the sole fillets and pat dry. Make a 1-inch-long (2.54 cm) cut at the thick part of each fillets and pull the fillet tip through the slit that has been created, so that a loop is made.

2. Briefly blanch the carrots and celery strips and chill them with cold water.

3. Grease a baking dish with ½ tablespoon butter, evenly distribute the vegetables on the bottom, and season lightly with salt and pepper.

4. Cut the fruits in half and squeeze out the juice. Use the back of a spoon to push the fruit through a fine strainer.

5. Season the fillets with salt and pepper and place them on the veg-

2 shallots, minced

1 tablespoon sweet butter

dash of chili powder

1 cup (¼ l) fresh coconut milk (page 15) or canned coconut milk

1 tablespoon chopped smooth-leaf parsley

pepper to taste

1. Cut the eggplant into 2-inch-thick (5 cm) slices and sprinkle with salt. Let the slices sit for 20 minutes on paper towels.

2. Skin off the monkfish's purplish outer membrane and cut the fish into 3-inch (7.6 cm) medallions. Trickle lemon juice over the fish.

3. Rinse off the eggplant slices, pat dry, and rub on the turmeric.

4. Heat the oil in a large skillet and fry the eggplant slices on both sides. They should remain light and not turn brown. Drain the slices on paper towels.

5. Melt the butter in a deep pot and sauté the garlic and the shallots for 3 minutes. Then sprinkle the chili powder over them and pour in the coconut milk.

6. Add the eggplant slices to the sauce and let the sauce simmer until it thickens. Remove the pot from the stove and sprinkle the parsley into the sauce.

7. Season the monfish medallions with salt and pepper, coat them in flour, and sauté them in the remaining 4 tablespoons of oil on both sides for 2 to 3 minutes until golden brown.

8. Serve the eggplant with the sauce and arrange the medallions on top.

etables. Flake the remaining ½ tablespoon of butter and distribute on the fish. Then pour on the fruit juice. Cover the baking dish with aluminum foil and cook the fish for 10 to 12 minutes.

6. Remove the baking dish from the oven, sprinkle the red peppercorns over everything and garnish with lemon balm or peppermint. Serve the fish in the sauce. Potatoes or rice go well with this meal.

Monkfish Medallions with Eggplants and Coconut Sauce

The subtle coconut flavor in this dish makes it distinctive.

Makes 4 servings

1 eggplant

salt

1½ pounds (600 g) monkfish

juice from 1 lemon

½ teaspoon turmeric powder

⅔ cup (140 ml) vegetable oil

1 clove of garlic, minced

Shrimp with Orange Noodles and Orange Sauce

This dish has great color appeal to match its great fresh orange taste.

Makes 4 servings

FOR THE NOODLES

zested peel of 1 organic orange
juice of 2 oranges
4 egg yolks
1 egg
pinch of salt
2 tablespoons olive oil
1 teaspoon finely cut tarragon
¾ cup (100 g) whole wheat flour
1¾ cups (200 g) all-purpose flour

FOR THE SAUCE

small piece of fresh ginger, peeled and minced
2 shallots, minced
1 carrot, diced
2 celery stalks, diced
1 teaspoon sweet butter
salt and white pepper to taste
juice from 3 oranges
½ cup (⅛ l) Fish Stock (page 47)
2 tablespoons sweet butter, chilled

FOR THE SHRIMP

12 large raw shrimp, unshelled, about 1 pound (454 g)
salt and white pepper to taste
¼ cup (60 ml) olive oil
½ clove garlic, minced
1 stem of fresh thyme, finely cut

1. For the noodle dough, reduce the orange peel and the orange juice in a pot over moderate heat until there is about 3 tablespoons of liquid, and then let cool.
2. Put the 4 egg yolks and the 1 egg into a bowl, add salt, and whisk everything until the eggs take on a darker color. Stir in the olive oil, reduced orange juice, and tarragon.
3. First blend in the whole wheat flour and gradually add the white flour. Knead the dough into a smooth, firm ball. If the dough is too soft, work some flour into it.
4. Fold the noodle into wax paper and let it rest for about 30 minutes in the refrigerator.
5. Melt the butter in a pot and add the ginger. Then add the shallots, carrots, and celery, and sauté everything for 5 minutes.
6. Pour in the orange juice and reduce over low heat to about half the amount. Then pour in the fish stock and let the liquid cook down to half the amount.

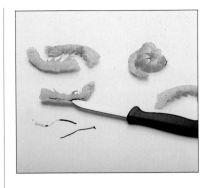

7. Thinly roll out the noodle dough on a work surface covered with flour. Cut the dough into thin strips. Cook the noodles in plenty of salted water until soft enough to eat. Drain in a colander.
8. Cut the shrimp in half lengthwise and devein the back side. Wash the shrimp and pat dry.
9. Heat the olive oil in a large skillet and sauté the shrimp on the cut side for 1 to 2 minutes. Add the garlic and the thyme.
10. Use two forks to twist the orange noodles into small nests and place them on deep plates. Arrange the shrimp halves around the noodles.
11. Cut 2 tablespoons of cold butter into cubes and stir into the simmering sauce. Season the sauce with salt and pepper and pour it over the shrimp.

Shrimp in Saffron Dough with Cherimoya Sauce

A lovely summer meal, the piquant, cold dipping sauce provides a nice contrast to the crispy shrimp.

Makes 4 servings
FOR THE DOUGH
1 to 1¼ cups (125 to 140 g) all-purpose flour
⅔ cup (150 ml) dry white wine
1 tablespoon oil
pinch of salt
pinch of granulated sugar
2 to 3 dashes of saffron powder
1 egg yolk
1 egg white

FOR THE SAUCE
1 cherimoya
2 shallots, minced
1 clove of garlic, minced
1 teaspoon sweet butter
½ cup (⅛ l) dry white wine
salt and white pepper to taste
1 teaspoon honey
3 to 4 drops Tabasco sauce
½ cup (100 g) Crème Fraîche (page 47) or sour cream

IN ADDITION
24 extra large shrimps, 2 to 3 ounces (50 to 60 g) each, shelled and deveined
juice from ½ lemon
seasonal salad greens for garnishing
3 cups (¾ l) vegetable oil for deep frying
salt and white pepper to taste
4 tablespoons all-purpose flour
2 lemons

1. For the dough, sift the flour into a bowl. Mix the wine with the oil, salt, sugar, saffron powder, and egg yolk, and stir the liquid into the flour. The dough should be smooth and viscous. Let the dough rest for about 30 minutes in the refrigerator.

2. Halve the cherimoya, scrape out the pulp with a spoon (see page 13), and pass it through a strainer, using the back of a spoon to push it through.

3. Heat the butter in a pot and sauté the shallots and the garlic for 3 minutes. Add the cherimoya and quench everything with white wine. Let the sauce cook down to half the amount, and season it with salt, pepper, honey, and Tabasco. Then pass it through a strainer and refrigerate it for 15 minutes.

4. Trickle lemon juice over the shrimp.

5. Beat the egg white stiff and blend it into the saffron dough.

6. Heat the oil very hot in a deep fat fryer or deep pot.

7. Coat the shrimp in flour and use a fork to dredge them in the saffron dough. Deep fry the shrimp until golden brown.

8. Mix the cold cherimoya sauce with the crème fraîche or sour cream and season it again with salt, pepper, and Tabasco.

9. Cut the lemon into pieces or slices and serve them with the shrimp. Garnish with salad greens and serve with the cherimoya sauce. Trickle lemon juice on each shrimp before dipping it into the cold sauce.

Shrimp Kabobs with Mango Rice

This simple dish has the look and flavor of a Caribbean meal.

Makes 4 servings
FOR THE RICE
1 firm mango
1 medium onion, finely chopped
1 cup (200 g) long grain white rice, uncooked
1½ cups (400 ml) Chicken Stock (page 46) or canned chicken broth

3 tablespoons sweet butter
1 bay leaf
pinch of salt

FOR THE KABOBS
12 extra large shrimp, 1.7 to 2
ounces (50 to 60 g) each, peeled
12 to 16 canned pearl onions
salt and white pepper to taste
6 tablespoons vegetable oil

1. Preheat the oven to 350°F (180°C).
2. Peel the mangos, cut the pulp off the stone (page 26), and cut into ³/₈-inch (1 cm) cubes.

3. Melt 2 tablespoons of butter in an oven-safe pot and sauté the onion until transparent. Add the rice and sauté it until it becomes glassy, stirring frequently.
4. Add the mango slices, stir everything, and pour in the chicken stock. Add the bay leaf and some salt, and cover the pot. Place the pot in the oven and cook the mango rice for about 20 minutes (do not stir).
5. In the meantime, cut the shrimps lengthwise and devein the back sides. Skewer them alternately with the pearl onions.

6. Remove the rice from the oven (it is done when the entire liquid has boiled away) and put it into a bowl. Crumble the remaining table-spoon of butter and blend it into the rice. Cover the pot to keep the mango rice warm.
7. Heat the oil in a large frying pan. Season the shrimp kabobs with salt and pepper and cook them for 4 to 6 minutes, turning once. Arrange the mango rice on plates and serve with the kabobs.

Pastries

Whether you are preparing for a special brunch or a festive buffet, you are certain to please family and friends with the following sweet delights.

Lemon Muffins with Dates

These muffins make a healthy dessert or a quick and nourishing breakfast.

Makes 12 muffins
2 ⅔ cups (250 g) oat bran
⅓ cup finely chopped almonds
4 dates, diced
1 tablespoon baking powder
2 tablespoons brown sugar
juice and zested peel from ½ organic lemon
1 cup (¼ l) milk
2 tablespoons vegetable oil
2 egg whites
2 tablespoons confectioners' sugar
some lemon juice

1. Preheat the oven to 400°F (200°C). Mix the oat bran with the almonds, the dates, the baking powder, and the sugar. Blend in the lemon juice and zested lemon.
2. Mix the milk with the oil and the egg whites. Add this mixture to the oat bran mixture and mix it quickly but thoroughly.
3. Place a dozen 2 to 2½ inch (5 to 6 cm) paper muffin tins on a baking sheet and carefully fill the paper tins with dough. Bake the muffins for 15 to 18 minutes.
4. In the meantime, mix the confectioners' sugar with some lemon juice and stir until smooth. When the muffins are done, frost them with this sugar mixture and let them cool.

Little Fruit Tarts with Lemon Cream

Try these with seasonal berries.

Makes 12 little tarts

FOR THE SHORTCAKE DOUGH
1¼ cups (150 g) all-purpose flour
¼ cup (50 g) granulated sugar
pinch of salt
zested peel from ½ organic lemon
1 teaspoon pure vanilla extract
½ cup (100 g) sweet butter
1 egg

FOR THE LEMON CREAM
¼ cup (65 g) sweet butter
⅓ cup (65 g) granulated sugar
juice and zest from 1 organic lemon
1 egg
4 to 5 tablespoons whipped cream

FOR THE FRUIT FILLING
1 kiwi
1 tamarillo
12 Cape gooseberries
1 small mango
¾ cup (80 g) fresh berries

IN ADDITION
sweet butter for tart tins
1 cup (¼ l) white wine
2 tablespoons granulated sugar
1 package apricoating (glaze)

1. Sift the flour onto the work surface and add the sugar, salt, lemon peel, and vanilla. Crumble the butter and distribute it on top of this mixture; then sift more flour over it. Mix the ingredients with a pastry blender or 2 knives until the dough is like coarse meal.

2. Make a groove in the middle, break the egg into it, and knead everything into a smooth dough.

3. Wrap the dough in aluminum foil and refrigerate for 30 minutes.

4. Combine the butter, sugar, lemon juice, and lemon peel in a pot and bring to a boil. Stir in the egg, let the mixture thicken and curdle, but do not let it boil anymore. Then pour everything through a fine strainer into a bowl and refrigerate.

5. On a floured work surface, roll out the dough ⅛ inch (0.3 cm) thick. Using a cookie-cutter form, cut out 12 circles, each about 5 inches (12 cm) in diameter. Grease a dozen 4-inch (10 cm) tart tins with butter. Spoon the dough into the tins. Prick the bottom of the dough with a fork several times and refrigerate for 15 minutes. Preheat the oven to 350°F (180°C).

6. Bake the tart shells for 12 to 15 minutes. Let them cool for about 5 minutes in the tins, then flip them over and let them cool on a rack.

7. Peel the kiwi and tamarillo (see page 22 and page 44), cut them into slices, and halve the slices. Take the Cape gooseberries out of the calyxes (see page 12) and slice them. Peel the mango, halve it, and remove the stone (see page 26).

8. Whisk the lemon cream and blend in the whipped cream. Distribute the cream in the tart shells, generously layer them with fruits, and refrigerate.

9. Combine the white wine and the sugar in a pot and bring to a boil. Stir in the apricoating, let cool, and coat the fruits with this glaze.

Little Nut Tarts with Mixed Fruit

The nutty biscuit dough makes these simple fruit tarts quite distinctive.

⤳

Makes 10 tarts

FOR THE FRUIT LAYERS

¾ cup (80 g) purple seeded grapes
1 cup (100 g) berries of the season
1 tart apple
2 medium plums

FOR THE BISCUIT DOUGH

2 egg yolks
2 tablespoons granulated sugar
2 egg whites
8 tablespoons ground hazelnuts
1 tablespoon all-purpose flour
1 tablespoon cornstarch
10 paper tart forms for baking, 2 to 2½ inches (5 to 6 cm) in diameter
confectioners' sugar for dusting

1. Wash the grapes, halve them, and remove the seeds (see page 19). Wash the berries and let them drain. Peel the apple, cut out the core, and cut the fruit into thin slices. Wash the plums, halve them, and remove the stones. Cut the fruit into thin slices. Refrigerate all the fruit.
2. Preheat the oven to 350°F (180°C). Stir the egg yolks with 1 tablespoon of sugar until foamy. Whisk the egg whites until stiff and trickle in the other tablespoon of sugar. Blend the egg white mixture into the egg yolk mixture.
3. Blend in the hazelnuts. Sift the flour and the corn starch into the mixture and blend everything well. Fill the paper forms two-thirds full with dough.
4. Distribute the fruits on the biscuit shells, set the paper forms on a baking sheet, and bake for about

15 minutes. Let them cool; then dust with confectioners' sugar.

Coconut Ginger Fancy Cake

The fresh flavors of lime, coconut, and ginger combine with delicious results.

⤳

Makes a 9½-inch (24 cm) diameter cake

FOR THE DOUGH

3 egg yolks
juice and zest from 1 organic lemon
1 cup (125 g) confectioners' sugar
pinch of salt
¼ cup (50 g) melted sweet butter
3 egg whites
⅔ cup (75 g) all-purpose flour
6 tablespoons (50 g) cornstarch

FOR THE FILLING

1⅔ cup (400 ml) fresh (page 15) or canned coconut milk
4 egg yolks
⅓ cup (75 g) granulated sugar
2 tablespoons rum
1 tablespoon finely chopped crystallized ginger
grated peel from 1 organic lime
¾ cup (200 g) whipped sweet butter
sugar for the cloth
5 tablespoons grated coconut

1. Preheat the oven to 350°F (180°C). Start the dough by stirring the butter with the lemon juice, the lemon peel, ½ cup (100 g) of confectioners' sugar, and 1 pinch of salt until foamy. Gradually add the egg yolks and stir well.
2. Whisk the egg whites with the rest of the confectioners' sugar

until very stiff and blend into the egg yolk mixture.

3. Sift the flour and the cornstarch onto the mixture and carefully mix everything with a whisk—do not stir.

4. Cover the bottom of a springform baking pan with baking parchment paper, pour in the dough, and bake for 15 to 20 minutes.

5. Let the bottom of the cake cool in the form, then tilt it onto a kitchen towel that is sprinkled with sugar. Then, tear off the baking paper. Let the cake rest in this position for 2 to 3 hours.

6. In the meantime, begin the fill-

ing. Put the coconut milk into a pot and carefully let it boil over moderate heat to about half the amount.

7. Combine the egg yolks with the sugar, and rum in a metal bowl, pour in the hot coconut milk, and stir well. Heat the mixture in the top part of a double boiler over simmering water until it thickens. Do not let the mixture boil.

8. Combine the ginger and the lime peel and add to the egg and coconut mixture. Let cool.

9. Stir the butter until creamy and gradually stir in the egg and coconut mixture.

10. Slice off 3 layers of cake so that you wind up with 4 layers of equal width. Put one-third of the coconut cream aside and coat 3 of the layers with the remaining mixture. Place these on top of each other and put the fourth layer on top. Coat the surface of the fancy cake and the edges with the remaining coconut cream and let the cake cool for at least 30 minutes in the refrigerator. Lightly roast the grated coconut in a dry pan and let cool. Sprinkle the edges of the cake and the surface with the grated coconut.

Algerian Date Cake

Served lukewarm or chilled, this simple cake takes on added elegance (and calories!) when served with sabayone or whipped cream.

❧

Makes a 9½ inch (24cm) diameter cake
24 medium dates
4 ounces (110 g) peeled almonds
3½ ounces (100 g) peeled, unsalted, roasted peanuts
5 tablespoons granulated sugar (divided)
4 egg whites
1 tablespoon sweet butter

❧

1. Preheat the oven to 350°F (180°C). Remove the dates' stones and finely chop the dates. Chop the almonds and the peanuts, too, or coarsely reduce them to small pieces in a food processor.
2. In a bowl, combine the dates, the chopped nuts, and 3 tablespoons of sugar and mix well.
3. Whisk the egg whites until stiff while gradually trickling in the remaining 2 tablespoons of sugar. Blend this mixture into the date and nut mixture.
4. Grease a springform cake pan with butter and pour in the mixture. Bake for 30 to 45 minutes until nicely brown.

Blueberry Cake with Royal

The rich custard filling and generous layer of blueberries make this dessert a double delight.

❧

Makes a 9½ inch (24cm) diameter cake
FOR THE SHORTCAKE DOUGH
1½ cups (180 g) whole wheat flour
1 tablespoon confectioners' sugar
pinch of salt
½ teaspoon pure vanilla extract
grated peel from ½ organic lemon
½ cup (100 g) sweet butter, plus 1 teaspoon for greasing pan
1 egg

FOR THE ROYAL
9 egg yolks
½ cup (60 g) granulated sugar
1 teaspoon pure vanilla extract
1 tablespoon vanilla pudding powder
pinch of salt
1¼ cups (300 g) heavy cream
1 cup (200 ml) milk

FOR THE FRUIT LAYER
3 cups (400 g) fresh blueberries

FOR THE ICING
1 cup (¼ l) white wine
2 tablespoons granulated sugar
1 package apricoating (glaze)

❧

1. For the shortcake dough, sift the flour onto the work surface and add the confectioners' sugar, salt, vanilla, and lemon peel. Crumble the butter and scatter it over the mixture, then sift more flour over everything.
2. Cut in the butter and flour with a pastry blender or 2 knives until the dough is like coarse meal.
3. Press a groove in the middle, break the egg into it, and quickly knead everything until the dough is smooth.
4. Wrap the dough in aluminium foil and let it rest for 30 minutes in the refrigerator. Grease the springform pan with butter.
5. Preheat the oven to 325°F (170°C). Roll out the dough on a floured work surface. The dough should be about 2¼ inches (6 cm) larger in diameter than the bottom of the pan. Roll the dough onto the rolling pin and roll it off over the pan.
6. Now fit the dough into the pan so that it juts out about ¼ inch (5 mm) at the edge. Moisten the outer edge of the pan with some drops of water and press the dough edge that juts onto it. This prevents shrinking when you bake the crust.
7. Prick the bottom of the crust several times with a fork and bake in the oven for about 10 minutes.
8. For the royal, mix the egg yolks with sugar, vanilla, and pudding powder. Stir in the heavy cream and milk.
9. Pour the royal onto the partially baked crust and bake for about 20 minutes. Let it cool and remove the cake from the pan.
10. Wash the blueberries and let them drain well. Distribute them on the bottom of the cake.
11. Bring the wine to a boil. Combine the sugar and the apricoating and stir it into the wine. Brush the glaze evenly on the fruit.

Cherry Streusel

Serve this special version of a traditional crumb cake lukewarm, garnished with sweetened heavy cream.

Makes 12 servings

FOR THE LEAVENED DOUGH

2 cups (250 g) all-purpose flour
½ cube yeast
½ cup (⅛ l) lukewarm milk
3 tablespoons sweet butter, plus butter for greasing pan
2 tablespoons granulated sugar
pinch of salt
1 egg
zested peel from ½ organic lemon

FOR THE FRUIT LAYER

1 cup (¼ l) milk
1½ tablespoons cornstarch
½ teaspoon pure vanilla extract
3 egg yolks
1 tablespoon confectioners' sugar
4 cups fresh cherries
⅓ cup (60 g) marzipan paste

FOR THE STREUSEL

2¾ cups (350 g) all-purpose flour
1 cup (200 g) sweet butter
1 cup (200 g) granulated sugar
1 teaspoon pure vanilla extract

1. To make the dough, sift the flour into a bowl, press a groove in the middle, and crumble the yeast into it. Add the milk and stir.
2. Cover everything with a thin layer of flour. Place a cloth over the bowl. Let the dough rise for 45 minutes in a warm place.
3. Melt the butter and add it to the remaining dough ingredients. Add this mixture to the leavened dough. Stir the dough with a wooden spoon until it bubbles.
4. Form the dough into a ball, cover it with a cloth, and let it rise in a warm spot for 15 minutes or until it has doubled in size.
5. For the fruit layer, mix 2 tablespoons of milk with the cornstarch. Mix the remaining milk with the vanilla and bring the mixture to a boil. Add the dissolved cornstarch to thicken it. Remove the milk mixture from the stove. Whisk the egg yolks and stir them in (the milk mixture should not be boiling). Sift confectioners' sugar thinly over the mixture so that it does not develop a skin as it cools. Let the milk mixture cool and become firm.
6. Wash the cherries, let them drain, and remove the stones.
7. Crumble the marzipan paste and slowly work the milk mixture into the marzipan with the kneading attachment of a hand mixer. Preheat the oven to 425°F (220°C). Grease the baking pan with butter. Knead the leavened dough one more time on a floured work surface, roll it out and cover the baking pan with it. Press an edge all around it.
8. Spread the marzipan paste onto the dough. Place the cherries on the paste and the cake. Let it rest for 10 to 15 minutes.
9. Mix the ingredients for the streusel and knead them loosely. Rub everything between your fingers until crumbs are formed.
10. Distribute the crumbs on the cake and bake for 35 to 40 minutes. Let the cake cool and cut it into rectangles.

Cherry and Hazelnut Cake

This hearty cake tastes wonderful served lukewarm, with a generous dollop of whipped cream, scented with cherry liqueur or rum.

Makes a 10-inch (26 cm) diameter cake

3 cups (750 g) fresh cherries
10 egg yolks

1 cup (200 g) granulated sugar

pinch of salt

3½ ounces (100 g) ground hazelnuts

¼ cup (50 g) candied orange peel, cubed

¼ cup (50 g) candied lemon peel, cubed

dash of powdered clove

1½ teaspoons powdered cinnamon

3 tablespoons (40 g) grated dark chocolate

2½ cups (240 g) bread crumbs (divided)

4 tablespoons cherry liqueur or rum

6 tablespoons red wine

10 egg whites

sweet butter for greasing pan

1. Preheat the oven to 350°F (170°C). Wash the cherries, let them drain, and remove the stones.

2. Combine the egg yolks and the sugar and stir until foamy. Stir in salt, hazelnuts, candied orange and lemon peel cubes, clove, cinnamon, and chocolate.

3. Soak three-quarters of the bread crumbs with the cherry liqueur or rum and the red wine and add to the dough. Whisk the egg whites until stiff and blend into the mixture.

4. Grease a springform pan with butter and strew the remaining bread crumbs evenly into it.

5. Blend the cherries into the dough, pour the dough into the pan and bake in the oven for 45 to 60 minutes. Should the surface get dark too soon, cover the pan with a piece of baking parchment paper.

6. After baking, take the cake out of the pan, let it cool, and cut it into slices.

Mango Strudel

If you are pressed for time, you can make this traditional Austrian dessert with ready-made phyllo sheets.

Makes 4 servings
FOR THE STRUDEL DOUGH
1⅔ cups (200 g) flour
½ cup (⅛ l) lukewarm water
½ tablespoon vegetable oil
pinch of salt

FOR THE FILLING
2 ripe mangos
1 tablespoon sweet butter
1 cup (100 g) fresh bread crumbs
⅓ cup (65 g) granulated sugar (divided)
1 teaspoon pure vanilla extract
4 tablespoons (50 g) heavy cream
4 tablespoons (50 g) melted sweet butter
5 tablespoons roasted finely sliced almonds
sweet butter for greasing the pan
confectioners' sugar for dusting

1. Sift the flour into a bowl and work it into a smooth dough with the water, oil, and salt. Knead the dough until it is soft and supple. Form the dough into a ball and place it in a deep plate moistened with oil. Cover the dough with plastic wrap and let it rest for 1 hour at room temperature.
2. For the filling, peel the mangos, halve them, and remove the stones (see page 26). Cut the pulp into ⅜-inch thick (1 cm) cubes.

3. Melt the butter in a skillet and roast the bread crumbs until they are golden yellow and nearly dry. Sprinkle 1 tablespoon of sugar over them and set aside on a plate.
4. Whisk the heavy cream until stiff, gradually blending in the rest of the sugar and the vanilla. Refrigerate the vanilla whipped cream.
5. Preheat the oven to 425°F (220°C). Roll the dough out very thinly on a cloth covered with flour. You should be able to see the cloth through the dough. Quickly and carefully brush the dough with some of the melted butter.
6. Mix the mango cubes with the sugared bread crumbs and the sliced almonds. Place half the fruit mixture along one short end of the strudel dough. Spread the vanilla whipped cream on top of the fruit filling and distribute the remainder of the mango mixture on top of the cream.
7. Fold over the sides on top of the filling. Lifting the towel to help you, roll up the filling along the long side to make a roll; do not roll the strudel too tightly.
8. With spatulas, carefully transfer the strudel onto a buttered baking sheet and brush the top with the remaining melted butter. Bake for about 20 minutes or until golden brown.
9. Let the strudel rest and cool for a few minutes after baking, then dust it with confectioners' sugar, and cut it into portions. Serve with vanilla sauce or passion fruit sabayone (see page 128).

Apricot Tart

Serve this eye-pleasing tart hot, topped with chilled sabayone or frozen yogurt.

Makes a 9-inch (23 cm) diameter tart
9-inch (23 cm) frozen pie crust
¾ cup (100 g) marzipan paste
some confectioners' sugar for rolling out
¼ cup (50 g) ground almonds
4 apricots
7 tablespoons (100 g) heavy cream
1 tablespoon granulated sugar
2 tablespoons apricot marmalade

1. Defrost the pie crust.
2. Roll the marzipan out on a little bit of confectioners' sugar and cover the bottom of the pie dough with it. Prick the bottom of the dough several times with a fork and sprinkle the almonds over it. Cover the pie with plastic wrap and refrigerate for 10 minutes.
3. Preheat the oven to 350°F (180°C). Remove the skin from the apricots, halve them, and remove the stones. Cut each half into 2 pieces.
4. Cover the bottom of the dough with apricots. Combine the heavy cream and the sugar in a pot and bring to a boil. Let the sugared cream boil down to about half the amount and pour it over the fruit.
5. Bake the tart on the lowest rack for about 20 minutes.
6. In the meantime, heat the apricot marmalade with 1 to 2 tablespoons of water and stir smooth. Cover the baked and still hot tart with the marmalade and serve.

Strawberry and Quince Cream Roll

This pretty dessert tastes like strawberry shortcake in a roll!

Makes 1 roll
FOR THE DOUGH
8 egg yolks
½ cup (100 g) granulated sugar (divided)
pinch of salt
zested peel from ½ organic lemon
4 egg whites
⅔ cup (80 g) all-purpose flour
1 tablespoon cornstarch

FOR THE FILLING
1 envelope strawberry gelatine
2 cups (400 ml) quince juice (if not available from a health-food store, substitute apple juice)
1 cup (150 g) fresh strawberries
1¾ cups (400 g) heavy cream

IN ADDITION
refined crystallized sugar
confectioners' sugar for dusting

1. Preheat the oven to 425°F (220°C). Cover a baking sheet with parchment baking paper.

2. To make the biscuit dough, vigorously stir the egg yolks with half the sugar, the salt, and the zested lemon. Whisk the egg whites until stiff, gradually adding the remaining sugar. Blend the egg white mixture into the egg yolk mixture.

3. Sift the flour and the corn starch over the mixture and blend well. With a spatula, spread the biscuit dough thinly onto the baking sheet. Bake in the oven for 8 to 12 minutes. Dissolve the gelatine in ¼ cup cold water.

4. Sprinkle a moistened kitchen towel with refined crystallized sugar and turn the baked dough upside down onto it. Moisten the parchment paper slightly with water and tear it off. Roll the biscuit into the cloth and let it cool.

5. In the meantime, put the quince juice into a pot and let it boil down to about ½ cup (100 ml).

6. Add the dissolved gelatine to the simmering juice and stir well. Let the juice cool.

7. Wash the strawberries and cut them into little pieces. Whisk the heavy cream until stiff. Shortly before the quince juice begins to turn into jelly, carefully blend in the cream.

8. Roll the dough out of the cloth, spread the quince-juice cream onto it, and distribute the strawberries on top. With the cloth to help you, again form the biscuit into a roll. Refrigerate the roll for 30 minutes or until it hardens. Dust it with confectioners' sugar and serve cold.

Tamarillo Yogurt Roll

The pleasantly bitter flavors of tamarillos and semisweet chocolate are mellowed with sweet cream and yogurt to create a tantalizing treat.

Makes 1 roll
FOR THE BISCUIT DOUGH
8 egg yolks
½ cup (100 g) granulated sugar (divided)
pinch of salt
zested peel of ½ organic lemon
4 egg whites
⅔ cup (80 g) all-purpose flour
1 tablespoon cornstarch

FOR THE FILLING
4 tamarillos
¾ cup (150 g) granulated sugar
juice from ½ lime
1 envelope unflavored gelatine
2 ounces (60 g) semisweet chocolate
½ cup (100 g) plain yogurt
1 cup (250 g) heavy cream

IN ADDITION
refined crystallized sugar
confectioners' sugar for dusting

1. Preheat the oven to 425°F (220°C). Cover a baking sheet with parchment baking paper.
2. To make the biscuit dough, vigorously stir the egg yolks with half the sugar, the salt, and the zested lemon. Whisk the egg whites until stiff, gradually adding the remaining sugar. Blend the egg white mixture into the egg yolk mixture.
3. Sift the flour and the cornstarch over the mixture and blend well. With a spatula, spread the biscuit dough thinly onto the baking sheet. Bake in the oven for 8 to 12 minutes. Dissolve the gelatine in ¼ cup cold water.
4. Sprinkle a moistened kitchen towel with refined crystallized sugar and turn the baked dough upside down onto it. Moisten the parchment paper slightly with water and tear it off. Roll the biscuit into the cloth and let it cool.
5. In the meantime, peel the tamarillos (see page 44) and cut them into cubes. Combine them with the sugar and the lime juice in a pot and let the fruit mixture boil until it thickens.
6. Pass the tamarillos through a strainer into a bowl, using the back of a spoon to push the fruit through. Add the dissolved gelatine and stir well. Let the tamarillo mixture cool.
7. Grate the chocolate into chips and refrigerate.
8. Stir the yogurt into the chilled tamarillo mixture and let it rest until almost firm.
9. Whisk the heavy cream until stiff, blend it into the tamarillo-yogurt mixture, and sprinkle in the cold chocolate chips.
10. Roll the dough out of the cloth and spread the mixture onto it. Then form the biscuit roll with the help of the cloth. Let the roll chill and harden in the refrigerator for 1 to 2 hours, then dust it with confectioners' sugar, and serve cold.

Mango Raspberry Charlotte

Presented uncut and garnished with whipped cream, this beautiful and scrumptious charlotte will be the highlight of any festive event.

Makes 1 dome cake
FOR THE DOUGH
4 egg yolks
¼ cup (50 g) granulated sugar (divided)
pinch of salt
zested peel from ½ organic lemon
2 egg whites
½ cup (50 g) all-purpose flour

FOR THE FILLING
1 ripe mango
3 tablespoons granulated sugar
½ cup (⅛ l) dessert wine (Muscatel)
1 envelope unflavored gelatine
⅔ cup (125 g) plain yogurt
¼ cup (80 g) heavy cream
1 cup (100 g) raspberries

IN ADDITION
refined crystallized sugar
⅔ cup (200 g) apricot marmalade (divided)
1 tablespoon orange liqueur

1. Preheat the oven to 425°F (220°C). Cover a baking sheet with parchment baking paper.

2. To make the biscuit dough, vigorously stir the egg yolks with half the sugar, the salt, and the zested lemon. Whisk the egg whites until stiff, gradually adding the remaining sugar. Blend the egg white mixture into the egg yolk mixture.

3. Sift the flour and the cornstarch over the mixture and blend well. With a spatula, spread the biscuit dough thinly onto the baking sheet. Bake in the oven for 6 to 8 minutes.

4. Sprinkle a moistened kitchen towel with refined crystallized sugar and turn the baked dough upside down onto it. Moisten the parchment paper slightly with water and tear it off. Cover the hot biscuit with ⅓ cup (100 g) apricot marmalade. Then, with the help of the cloth, roll up the dough and let it cool.

5. Peel the mango, cut it in half, and remove the stone (see page 26). Cut the pulp into small cubes and combine them with the sugar and the wine in a pot and cook until soft. Puree the fruit mixture with a hand or electric blender and let the mango purée boil until it thickens.

6. Dissolve the gelatine in ¼ cup cold water. Pass the purée through a strainer, using the back of a spoon to push the fruit through.

7. Blend the dissolved gelatine into the still hot mango purée. Let the mixture cool, stir in the yogurt, and let the filling rest until almost firm.

8. In the meantime, cover the inside of a dome-shaped cake pan with plastic wrap. Cut the biscuit roll into about ¼-inch-thick (5 mm) slices and densely cover the bottom of the pan. Set aside 4 or 5 biscuit slices for what will become the bottom of the charlotte.

9. Whisk the heavy cream until stiff and blend it into the filling shortly before it becomes firm.

10. Wash the raspberries, pat them dry, and stir them into the filling. Pour the filling onto the biscuit slices in the pan, up to ⅜ inch (1 cm) below the edge. Refrigerate the cake for about 20 minutes.

11. Cover the top of the cake with the remaining biscuit slices, cover it with plastic wrap, and refrigerate the charlotte for 1 to 1½ hours.

12. Stir the remaining ⅓ cup (100 g) apricot marmalade until smooth with the orange liqueur and warm it up.

13. Remove the plastic wrap from the top of the charlotte and turn the cake upside down onto a platter, tearing off the remaining plastic wrap. Spread the marmalade onto what is now the top of the cake. Cut the charlotte into slices and serve cold.

Desserts

With the increasing availability of so many types of fruit, it is now possible to create a wide variety of inventive dessert recipes that combine local and exotic fruits.

Exotic Fruit Salad

The eye-pleasing combination of local and tropical fruits makes this a tasty treat.

Makes 4 to 6 servings
1 pink grapefruit
2 oranges
1 mango
1 small honeydew melon
2 mangosteens
1 tamarillo
1 kiwi
2 tablespoons white rum
4 tablespoons Purified Sugar (page 47)
some fresh peppermint leaves, cut into fine strips

1. Peel the grapefruit and the oranges, cut out the segments (see page 31), and squeeze the juice out of the fruit walls into a bowl.
2. Peel the mango, cut it in half, and remove the stone (see page 26). Cut the fruit into slices. Cut the melon in half, remove the seeds, and scoop out little balls (see page 28). Peel the mangosteen and divide the fruit into individual segments (see page 27). Peel the tamarillo (see page 44) and the kiwi and cut both into slices.
3. Add the rum to the citrus juices and mix in the purified sugar. Stir in the peppermint.
4. Arrange the fruits on plates, pour the marinade over them, and refrigerate for about 15 minutes. Serve chilled.

Rum-Flavored Plums with Two Kinds of Chocolate Mousse

Here's a real chocolate lover's dessert: calorie-counters beware!

Marinating time: at least 12 hours
Cooling time: about 2 hours
Makes 4 servings

FOR THE RUM-FLAVORED PLUMS
15 medium plums
1½ cups (300 g) granulated sugar
⅔ cup (150 ml) rum
½ cinnamon stick
½ cup (⅛ l) dry red wine

FOR THE DARK MOUSSE
7 ounces (200 g) dark chocolate
2 ½ ounces (50 g) milk chocolate
2 cups (450 g) heavy cream
3 egg whites
2 tablespoons rum

FOR THE LIGHT MOUSSE
9 ounces (250 g) white chocolate
1 cup (250 g) heavy cream
3 egg whites
1 envelope unflavored gelatine
2 tablespoons Grand Marnier

FOR GARNISHING
shaved dark chocolate
finely chopped nuts or pistachios

1. Wash the plums and let them drain. Cut them into quarters and remove the pits. Put the plums in a pot with the sugar, rum, and cinnamon stick, and let them sit for 30 minutes.

2. Add the red wine to the plum mixture and bring to a boil, stirring continuously. Remove any foam. Take the pot off the stove, cover it with a lid, and let the plums marinate for 12 hours or overnight.

3. For the dark mousse, cut the chocolate into small pieces and melt them in the top part of a double boiler over simmering water. Do not let the chocolate get too hot.

4. Whisk the heavy cream until stiff and put it aside. Whisk the egg whites.

5. Pour the rum into the chocolate and stir well. Blend in the egg whites and gradually mix in the whipped cream. These steps have to be done quickly, because the chocolate cools off fast. Pour the mousse into a bowl, cover it, and refrigerate for about 2 hours.

6. Prepare the white mousse in the same way, using the ingredients indicated. The only difference is that you will add the envelope of gelatine (dissolved in ¼ cup cold water). Refrigerate this mousse for 2 hours, also.

7. Place one scoop of each kind of mousse onto plates and serve with the rum-flavored plums. Garnish the dessert with chocolate shavings and/or nuts.

Red Wine Pears

To celebrate the apple harvest in the autumn, try this recipe with sweet apples.

❧

Marinating time: 1 day
Makes 4 servings
3 cups (³⁄₄ l) dry red wine
juice from ¹⁄₂ lemon
juice from 1 orange
2 whole cloves
¹⁄₂ cinnamon stick
2 allspice seeds
dash of powdered ginger
³⁄₄ cup (150 g) granulated sugar
4 pears with stems
3 egg yolks
8 small scoops of vanilla, chocolate, or caramel ice cream
fresh mint leaves for garnishing

❧

1. In a pot, combine the red wine with the lemon juice and the orange juice. Add the spices and the sugar and bring to a boil.
2. Peel the pears but do not remove the stems. Cut them in half, cut through the stem in the middle, and cut out the cores.
3. Place the pear halves into the boiling red wine and simmer over low heat. The pears should not get too soft.
4. Take the pot from the stove, cover it with a lid, and let the pears marinate for 1 day.
5. The next day, let the marinated pears drain in a colander over a bowl to catch the red wine mixture. Cut the pears in a fanlike shape.
6. Whisk ¹⁄₂ cup (¹⁄₈ l) of the red wine mixture with the 3 egg yolks

in the top part of a double boiler over lightly boiling water until you achieve a thick sabayone consistency. Lower the heat so that the water is simmering and continue to whisk the mixture until it cools down.
7. Arrange two pear fans on each plate, pour some red wine sabayone onto the plate, and add 2 small scoops of ice cream. Garnish the dessert with mint leaves.

Dates Filled with White Mocha Sauce with Pineapple Ice Cream

This recipe takes time and patience, but the results are worth it.

❧

Freezing time: about 3 hours
Makes 4 servings
FOR THE SAUCE
1¹⁄₄ cups (300 ml) milk
¹⁄₂ cup (80 g) granulated sugar
3 tablespoons roasted espresso coffee beans
4 egg yolks
2 tablespoons whipped cream

FOR THE ICE CREAM
1 large pineapple without skin (page 37)
1 cup (237 ml) milk
¹⁄₂ cup (125 g) heavy cream
4 egg yolks
3 tablespoons sugar

FOR THE DATES
20 fresh dates
³⁄₄ cup (100 g) raw marzipan paste

2 tablespoons confectioners' sugar
2 tablespoons cherry liquor
1¹⁄₂ ounces (50 g) grated pistachio nuts

FOR GARNISHING
fresh peppermint leaves
finely chopped nuts and/or chocolate shavings

❧

1. Combine the milk, sugar, and espresso beans in a pot and bring to a boil. Take the pot off the stove and let the beans sit in the sauce for 10 minutes. Then it through a fine strainer into a bowl.
2. For the ice cream, cut half the pineapple into small cubes. Chop the rest of the fruit and combine it with the sugar and 2 tablespoons of water in a pot. Heat the pineapple for 3 minutes and then mash the mixture well. Add the pineapple cubes and let them cook over low heat for about 5 minutes.
3. Combine the milk and the heavy cream in a pot and bring to a boil.
4. In another pot, whisk the 4 egg yolks into the sugar until you achieve a creamy, but not foamy, mixture. Carefully pour the milk and cream mixture over the egg and sugar mixture, reheat briefly, stirring with a wooden spoon until the mixture is thoroughly blended and very creamy. While doing this, do not let the mixture boil.
5. Pour the ice cream mixture through a fine strainer into the pineapple mixture and mix well. Pour the ice cream into a metal bowl and place it covered in the freezer. After about 20 minutes, stir the ice cream well, then return it to the freezer. Stir it every 20 min-

utes (freezing time about 3 hours), until the ice cream is creamy.

6. Put the 4 egg yolks for the sauce into the top of a double boiler over lightly boiling water and stir until foamy. Add the mocha milk and whisk the sauce until creamy. Then pass the sauce through a fine strainer into a bowl and place it in the refrigerator.

7. Cut the dates open lengthwise up to the pit. Remove the pit with the tip of a knife, cut all the way through the date, and cut out the stem.

8. Knead the marzipan with the confectioner's sugar, Maraschino, and three-quarters of the pistachios. At first, form the mixture into small balls; then form long sausages.

9. Place the marzipan sausages onto the date halves and slightly press them in with your fingers. Sprinkle the dates with the remaining pistachios and refrigerate for 10 minutes.

10. Pour the mocha sauce into a blender and blend in the whipped cream.

11. Pour a generous amount of sauce into the middle of each plate, arrange the dates in a star shape on top, and place one large ball of pineapple ice cream in the middle of each plate. Garnish with peppermint leaves, chopped nuts and/or chocolate shavings.

Tip: If you own an ice cream machine, you can proceed from Step 5 on as follows: Pour the ice cream mixture into the machine and let it freeze until creamy. Then store the ice cream in the freezer.

Marinated Peaches with Raspberry Sabayone

Present this dessert with all the fanfare it deserves.

❧

Marinating time: 2 days
Makes 4 servings
FOR THE PEACHES
2 cups (½ l) medium dry white wine
2 tablespoons sugar
1 organic lemon
4 tablespoons peach liqueur
4 ripe peaches

FOR THE SABAYONE
2 cups (150 g) fresh raspberries
2 tablespoons confectioners' sugar
3 egg yolks
1 cup (100 g) whipped cream

FOR GARNISHING
chocolate shavings
2 tablespoons finely chopped pistachio nuts

1. Pour the wine into a pot and stir in the sugar. Peel the skin off the lemon in thin spirals. Squeeze the juice and add it and the peel spirals to the wine. Add the liquor and bring everything to a boil.
2. Dip the peaches briefly into boiling water, refrigerate them until cold, and peel off the skin. Put the fruits into a large bowl.
3. Pour the boiling wine liquid over the peaches so that the fruit is completely covered. Cover the bowl with plastic wrap and let the fruits marinate for 2 days.
4. Puree the raspberries in a food processor and pass them through a strainer into a metal bowl. Blend in the confectioners' sugar and the egg yolks. Transfer this mixture into the top of a double boiler over lightly boiling water and mix well. Pour in ½ cup (⅛ l) of the peach marinade and whisk until a creamy, firm sabayone is achieved.
5. Transfer the sabayone into a cold bowl and whisk until cold. Blend in 3 tablespoons of whipped cream.
6. Remove peaches from the marinade and let drain. Arrange the dessert as shown in the photo. Garnish with chocolate shavings and chopped pistachios.

Passion Fruit Sabayone

Here's a simple recipe for a favorite dessert.

❧

Makes 4 to 6 servings
6 passion fruits
juice from 2 oranges
6 egg yolks
⅔ cup (120 g) sugar
½ cup (⅛ l) dry white wine

1. Cut the passion fruits in half, scrape out the pulp with a spoon, and put it in a food processor. Add the orange juice and blend well. Pour the mixture into a pot and bring to a boil.
2. Pass the mixture through a strainer, using the back of spoon to push it through into a metal bowl. Let cool. Then, add the egg yolks, sugar, and white wine and stir thoroughly.
3. Place the mixture in the top part of a double boiler over lightly boiling water. Whisk the mixture until foamy.
4. Carefully pour the sabayone into bowls and serve it immediately.

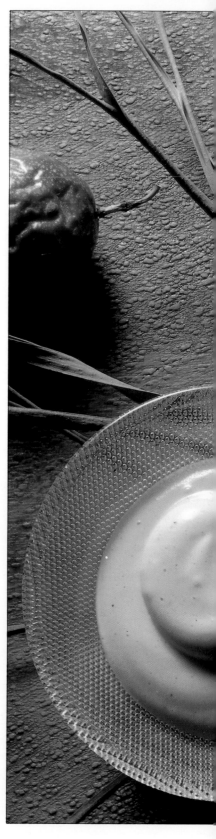

Fruit Sorbets

Light and flavorful alternatives to ice cream, sorbets can be made from a wide variety of fruits, accented with liqueurs or mineral water, as the following recipes demonstrate.

Pear Sorbet

Freezing time: about 2 hours
Makes 8 servings
1 teaspoon of unflavored gelatine
10 medium pears
juice from 1 lemon
2 tablespoons pear schnapps
sparkling wine, champagne, or pear schnapps to taste

1. Wash the pears, cut them into quarters, and cut out the cores. Cut the fruit with the skin into pieces.

2. Put the pear pieces into a food processor, add the lemon juice and the schnapps, and quickly blend everything into small pieces so that the fruit does not turn brown. Dissolve the gelatine in ¼ cup cold water and blend it into the mixture. Press the mixture through a fine strainer with the back of a spoon to remove any large pieces of skin.

3. Put the pear mixture into a metal bowl, cover it with plastic wrap, and put it in the freezer.

Remove the bowl after 20 minutes, stir in the ice crystals at the edges of the bowl and from the surface of the sorbet. Then return the bowl to the freezer.

4. Freeze the sorbet for a total of 2 hours, stirring every 20 minutes. It is ready to eat when it becomes creamy and frosted. For an even smoother and lighter sorbet, beat the frozen dessert with an electric or hand rotary beater just before serving.

5. To serve, either squirt the sorbet through a pastry bag with a star-shaped spout into chilled bowls or glasses or scoop out large balls of sorbet and put them in cold glasses. Pour sparkling wine, champagne, or pear schnapps over each serving, depending on your preferences.

Tangerine Sorbet

Freezing time: about 2 hours

Makes 8 servings

10 or 11 tangerines

¾ cup (200 ml) Purified Sugar (page 47)

grated peel from 2 organic oranges

juice from 1 lemon

½ cup (⅛ l) mineral water

tangerine segments or fresh peppermint leaves for garnishing

1. Squeeze the tangerines and pass the juice through a strainer. You should have about 2½ cups (600 ml) of juice. If necessary, squeeze more tangerines.
2. Mix the purified sugar with the tangerine juice, add the orange peel, and season the mixture with the lemon juice.
3. Put the tangerine mixture into a metal bowl, cover it with plastic wrap, and place it in the freezer. Remove it out after about 20 minutes, stir in the mineral water, and freeze it again for 20 minutes. Continue as described in the "Pear Sorbet" recipe above, Step 4 and Step 5. Garnish, to your liking, with tangerine segments or peppermint leaves.

Tamarillo Sorbet with Gin

Freezing time: about 2 hours

Makes 8 servings

10 ripe tamarillos

juice from 1 lime

juice from 2 blood oranges

¾ cup (200 ml) Purified Sugar (page 47)

½ cup (⅛ l) gin

some gin for garnishing

1. Peel the tamarillos (see page 44). Cut the fruit into pieces and blend the fruit in a food processor.
2. Mix the fruit purée with the lime juice and the orange juice. Blend in the purified sugar and the gin.
3. Freeze the mixture for about 2 hours in the freezer, stirring every 20 minutes as described in the previous two sorbet recipes, Step 4 and Step 5. If you like, pour a little gin over the sorbet when you serve it.

Tip: If you own a sorbet or ice cream maker, you can proceed after Step 3 of the last three recipes as follows: Pour the sorbet mixture into the machine and let it freeze until it becomes creamy. For the recipe "Tangerine Sorbet," add the mineral water as soon as the mixture begins to freeze.

Fruit Granita

Granita is similar to sherbet but is not as sweet and has a deliberately grainy texture.

Passion Fruit Granita

Freezing time: 3 hours
Makes 4 to 6 servings
12 passion fruits
⅔ cup (120 g) granulated sugar
juice from 2 oranges
14 ounces (400 ml) dry sparkling wine or champagne
fresh peppermint leaves for garnishing

1. Halve the passion fruits, scrape out the pulp with a spoon, pass it through a fine strainer, and catch the juice in a bowl. You should have about ½ cup (100 ml) of juice.
2. Put the sugar into a pot over low heat and caramelize slightly. Quench the mixture with passion fruit juice. Add the orange juice and dissolve the sugar in the liquid.
3. Let the mixture cool and pour it into a wide, shallow pan. Add the sparkling wine or champagne, carefully stir, and put it in the freezer.
4. Let the liquid freeze. From time to time, loosen the ice crystals at the edges and on the surface of the mixture, and stir gently. The more often you do this, the more finely grained the granita will become.
5. When the granita is completely frozen (about 3 hours), stir the mixture one more time, and spoon it into chilled bowls or glasses. Garnish with peppermint.

Pomegranate Granita

Freezing time: about 3 hours
Makes 4 to 6 servings
5 pomegranates
6 tablespoons grenadine
¼ cup (50 g) granulated sugar
2 cups (½ l) hearty red wine
3 organic limes

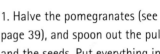

1. Halve the pomegranates (see page 39), and spoon out the pulp and the seeds. Put everything into a pot. Add the grenadine and the sugar and stir well. Pour in one-quarter of the red wine and stir.
2. Heat the liquid and let it simmer gently for 4 to 5 minutes. Use an electric or hand beater to mix it slightly; this is the best way to loosen the skins and the seeds. Use the back of a spoon to push the mixture through a strainer.
3. Let the mixture cool. Pour it into a wide, shallow pan. Add the rest of the wine. Squeeze 2 limes, add the juice, and stir carefully. Place the pan in the freezer.
4. Continue as described in "Passion Fruit Granita," Step 4.
5. Wash the last lime with hot water and cut it into very fine slices. Pour the granita into chilled bowls or glasses and garnish with the lime slices. Serve immediately.

Mango Raspberry Terrine

The "hot" colors of this delicious dessert are a great counterpoint to its cool taste.

~

Makes 8 servings
1 envelope unflavored gelatine
2 to 3 ripe mangos
3¼ cups (400 g) raspberries
¾ cup (250 g) plain yogurt
2 cups (150 g) whipped cream

~

1. In a pot, dissolve the gelatine in ¼ cup cold water.

2. Peel the mangos, halve them, and remove the stones (see page 26). Cut the fruit into very thin slices.
3. Carefully line a medium-size, rectangular baking pan with plastic wrap. Completely cover the bottom and sides of the pan with mango slices, making sure that the slices overlap slightly. Set aside enough mango slices to cover the top of the terrine later.
4. Put 1 cup (100 g) of the raspberries aside. Wash the rest, put them in a food processor, and reduce them to small pieces. Press them with the back of a spoon through a fine strainer into a bowl.

5. Blend in the gelatine. Shortly before the raspberry purée thickens, blend in the yogurt and the whipped cream.
6. Pour the mixture into the baking pan, place the washed raspberries that you set aside evenly on top, and cover the mixture evenly with the remaining mango slices.

7. Let the terrine cool in the refrigerator for 1 hour, then overturn it onto a platter and slice it carefully with a knife rinsed in hot water.
Tip: If you wish, you can serve the terrine with passion fruit sabayone (recipe page 128).

Sesame Parfait with Kumquat Sauce

The distinctive flavor and delicate crunch of sesame seeds are "parfait-ly" complemented by the tangy kumquat and orange sauce.

~

Freezing time: about 2 hours
Makes 8 servings
FOR THE SAUCE
13 medium kumquats
3 tablespoons granulated sugar

½ teaspoon pure vanilla extract
small piece of fresh ginger, finely chopped
juice from 4 oranges
juice from 1 organic lemon
fresh peppermint or lemon balm for garnishing

FOR THE PARFAIT
½ cup (100 g) granulated sugar (divided)
2 tablespoons sesame seeds
juice from 2 oranges
2 teaspoons sesame oil (divided)
½ teaspoon unflavored gelatine
3 egg yolks
1 egg
2⅓ cups (200 g) heavy cream

~

1. For the sauce, wash the kumquats, halve them, and press out the pits (see page 31). Cut the fruit halves into 2 or 4 pieces, depending on their size, and put them in a bowl. Blend in the sugar, vanilla, and ginger. Cover the bowl with plastic wrap and refrigerate.
2. For the parfait, melt 2 tablespoons sugar in a pot until it turns a caramel color. Then sprinkle in the sesame seeds, stir, and gradually pour in the orange juice. Slowly bring the liquid to a boil over moderate heat, stirring frequently.
3. Put the mixture into a baking dish that has been coated with about 1 teaspoon of sesame oil. Smooth the mixture flat and let it cool. Then break the sesame seeds into pieces and reduce to smaller pieces in a food processor.
4. Dissolve the gelatine in ¼ cup of cold water. Put the egg yolks, the egg, and ⅓ cup sugar into the top

part of a double boiler over lightly boiling water, and whisk the mixture until warm. Then transfer the mixture to a bowl, add 1 teaspoon of sesame oil, and stir the mixture with a hand or electric blender until it has cooled and increased in volume.

5. Add the dissolved gelatine to the sesame seed mixture and blend in the egg mixture. Whisk the heavy cream stiff and blend it into the parfait mixture. Fill 8 muffin tins with the parfait. Freeze for about 2 hours.

6. Pour the kumquats into a pot, add the orange juice, and slowly cook over moderate heat until the fruit is soft. Skim off the foam as necessary. Season the sauce with lemon juice and refrigerate.

7. Gently ease the parfaits onto plates and serve it with the kumquat sauce. Garnish, to your liking, with fresh mint or lemon balm leaves.

Tip: Reserve about 1 teaspoon of sesame seeds and sprinkle some onto each plate before serving.

Emperor's Scrambled Pancake with Cranberries

Add this famous Austrian dessert to your traditional Thanksgiving fare and get ready for rave reviews.

Makes 4 servings

FOR THE CRANBERRIES

2½ cups fresh or frozen cranberries
½ cup (100 g) granulated sugar
¼ cinnamon stick
dash of ginger powder
grated peel from ½ organic orange
½ cup (⅛ l) medium dry red wine
1 teaspoon cornstarch

FOR THE SCRAMBLED PANCAKE

1 cup (125 g) all-purpose flour
pinch of salt
4 egg yolks
1 cup (¼ l) milk
4 egg whites
2 tablespoons granulated sugar
2 tablespoons sweet butter
1 to 2 tablespoons raisins
1 tablespoon finely sliced almonds
confectioners' sugar for dusting

1. In a bowl, combine the cranberries, sugar, spice, and orange peel. Let the fruits draw juice for about 20 minutes.

2. Add the red wine and bring everything to a boil over moderate heat. Let the berries come to a full boil and then lower the heat and simmer for about 1 minute.

3. Dissolve the cornstarch in some water and thicken the fruit with it. Remove the cinnamon stick and let the berries cool.

4. For the pancakes, sift the flour and salt into a bowl. Add the egg yolks and the milk and blend the batter until smooth.

5. Preheat the oven to 350°F (180°C).

6. Whisk the egg whites until stiff and slowly trickle in the sugar. Blend the egg white mixture into the batter.

7. Melt half the butter in a large, ovenproof pan and pour in the pancake batter.

8. Bake the batter for 3 minutes, remove the pan from the oven and add the raisins. Return the pan to the oven and continue to bake the pancake until it starts to turn light brown. Then turn the pancake over with a spatula, crumble the remaining butter and distribute it around the edges of the pan. Continue to bake the pancake for about 5 more minutes.

9. Remove the pancake from the oven and scramble it into irregular pieces.

10. Strew almonds over the scrambled pancake, let the steam dissipate, and serve it on plates. Dust everything with confectioners' sugar and serve with the cranberries.

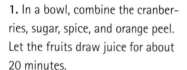

1. Sift the flour into a bowl and mix in the salt, wine, and egg yolks. Let the dough rest for about 30 minutes.

2. In the meantime, pick and wash the strawberries. Reserve 12 of the nicest and largest strawberries. Cut another 5 to 6 strawberries into strips and chop the remaining fruits into small pieces.

3. Put the small pieces of strawberries into a bowl and strew the confectioners' sugar over them. Puree the strawberries with a hand or electric blender and add the lemon juice. Pour the pulp into a strainer and use the back of a spoon to strain it into a bowl. Add the strips of strawberry, stir, and place the mixture in the refrigerator.

4. Heat the oil in a deep fryer or deep pot; the oil should be very hot.

5. Beat the egg whites until stiff and blend them into the dough. Coat the remaining whole strawberries in flour, stick each one onto a fork, and carefully pull each one through the dough.

6. Fry the strawberries until they are golden brown, turning them over frequently. Let them drain on paper towels. Mix the sugar with the cinnamon and roll the fried strawberries in the mix. The cinnamon–sugar should adhere to the strawberries on all sides.

7. Take the strawberry purée out of the refrigerator and add the peppermint strips and the sparkling wine or champagne. Stir thoroughly and ladle into deep plates. Serve the cold soup with 3 fried strawberries per person.

Chilled Strawberry Soup with Deep-Fried Strawberries

For added indulgence, serve the strawberry soup with a generous scoop of vanilla or strawberry ice cream.

Makes 4 servings
FOR THE DOUGH
1 cup (125 g) all-purpose flour plus 3 to 4 tablespoons
pinch of salt
½ cup (⅛) smooth white wine
2 egg yolks
2 egg whites

FOR THE SOUP
3½ cups (500 g) strawberries
2 tablespoons confectioners' sugar
juice from ½ lemon
2 stems of fresh peppermint, cut into fine strips
2 cups (½ l) dry sparkling wine or champagne

IN ADDITION
vegetable oil for deep frying
3 tablespoons granulated sugar
dash of cinnamon powder

Banana Soufflé with Chilled Cactus Pear Butter

Chilled fruit butter is a wonderful partner for this easy-to-make soufflé.

❧

Makes 4 servings

FOR THE CACTUS PEAR BUTTER
4 cactus pears
½ cup (100 g) granulated sugar
4 tablespoons whiskey
juice from 3 oranges
½ teaspoon pure vanilla extract
½ teaspoon cornstarch
3 tablespoons sweet butter, chilled

FOR THE SOUFFLÉ
¼ cup (60 g) sweet butter
½ cup (80 g) granulated sugar plus 3 tablespoons
3 egg yolks
2 large bananas
juice from 1 lemon
5 tablespoons roasted slivered almonds
3 tablespoons chocolate shavings
1 tablespoon cornstarch
3 egg whites
butter and sugar for the soufflé dishes
confectioners' sugar for dusting
peppermint leaves for garnishing

❧

1. Carefully peel the cactus pears (see page 11) and slice them.
2. Caramelize the sugar in a pot and quench it with whiskey and orange juice. Add the cactus pear slices and the vanilla. Simmer the sauce for about 5 minutes and then puree it in a food processor. Pass the pulp through a strainer.
3. Preheat the oven to 400°F (200°C).
4. For the soufflé, blend the butter with 2 tablespoons of sugar and gradually add the egg yolks.
5. Peel the bananas, cut them into small pieces, and puree them with the lemon juice in a food processor. Add the banana purée to the egg-butter mixture, and blend. Stir in the slivered almonds, the chocolate shavings, and the cornstarch.
6. Grease 4 soufflé dishes (about 2¾ inches/7 cm in diameter) with butter and dust them with sugar.
7. Whisk the egg white until stiff and slowly trickle in the remaining sugar. Gently blend the egg white mixture into the soufflé mixture and fill the soufflé dishes three-quarters full.
8. Place the dishes in an ovenproof pan and fill the pan almost to the top with simmering water. Place the pan in the oven and bake for 20 to 25 minutes. The temperature of the water should continue to simmer but must not boil.
9. Reheat the cactus pear butter and thicken it with cornstarch dissolved in a little bit of cold water. Crumble the cold butter and add it to the simmering sauce.
10. Pour the cactus pear butter into a metal bowl and place it on top of a larger bowl filled with water and ice cubes. Whisk the cactus pear butter until cold.
11. Distribute the cactus pear butter onto 4 plates. Gently lift the soufflés out of the dishes and arrange them on the sauce with the baked side facing up. Garnish with peppermint leaves, dust with confectioners' sugar, and serve immediately.

Exotic Fruit Gratin

The sweet and warm cream sauce is a wonderful complement to this exotic fruit medley.

Makes 4 servings
FOR THE GRATIN
2 kiwis
1 baby pineapple
2 figs
2 mangosteens
1 mango
1 persimmon
1 pomelo
*1 tablespoon confectioners' sugar
for dusting*

FOR THE SABAYONE
3 egg yolks
1/2 cup (100 g) granulated sugar
1/2 cup (1/8 l) medium sweet white wine

1. Peel the kiwis and cut each one into 6 slices. Peel the baby pineapple, cut it into quarters, cut out the stalk (see page 37) and cut the fruit into slices. Peel the figs (see page 18) and divide them into thick slices. Cut the mangosteen open and divide the fruit pulp into segments (see page 25).

2. Peel the mango, halve it, and remove the stone (see page 26). Cut the fruit into slices. Wash the persimmon and cut it into slices (see page 36). Peel the pomelo and cut out the segments (see grapefruit, page 21). Arrange the fruits on 4 ovenproof plates.

3. For the sabayone, put the egg yolks into a metal bowl, trickle in the sugar, and add the wine. Pour the mixture into the top part of a double boiler over lightly boiling water and whisk gently until the sabayone becomes foamy. Then vigorously whisk the sabayone until it becomes a homogeneous, foamy batter.

4. Pour the sabayone over the fruits and broil until the gratin turns golden brown. Dust everything with confectioners' sugar and serve immediately.

Tip: If you do not have a broiler, you can bake the gratin in a preheated oven at 475°F (250°C).

Recipe Index

Algerian Date Cake 112
Apricot Tart 117
Avocado Buttermilk Soup with Salmon Cakes 61
Avocado Orange Salad with Raspberry Vinaigrette 50

Bacon-Seasoned Pike with Banana-Peanut Butter Sauce 88
Banana Souffle with Chilled Cactus Pear Butter 138
Beef Stock 46
Beef Tenderloin with Papaya and Ginger 73
Blueberry Cake with Royal 112

Calf's Tongue and Tangerine Salad with Lemon Balm Vinaigrette 50
Cherry and Hazelnut Cake 114
Cherry Streusel 114
Chicken Breast with Curried Fruits and Grated Coconut 68
Chicken in Spicy Coconut Sauce 69
Chicken Liver Pate with Fig Confit 59
Chicken Stock 46
Chicken with Kumquats 72
Chicken with Nectarines and Scallions 71
Chilled Strawberry Soup with Deep-Fried Strawberries 137
Coconut Ginger Fancy Cake 110
Cod with Horseradish Crust and Cactus Pear Sauce 92
Cod with Pineapple 94
Creamed Melon Soup 62
Crème Frache 47

Dates Filled with White Mocha Sauce with Pineapple Ice Cream 126

Emperor's Scrambled Pancake with Cranberries 136
Exotic Fruit Gratin 140
Exotic Fruit Salad 124

Fish Stock 47
Flounder and Salmon Roulade with Cherimoya Sauce 91

Halibut Steak in Vegetable Sauce with Fried Fruit 98
Ham Ragout with Pineapple 78
Hot Apple Soup 65

Lamb Curry in Lemon Sauce 83
Lamb Medallions with Seville Orange Sauce 82
Lamb Shanks in Cranberry Red Wine Sauce 80
Lemon Chicken 70
Lemon Muffins with Dates 108
Lemon Soup 63
Little Fruit Tarts with Lemon Cream 109
Little Nut Tarts with Mixed Fruit 110

Mahi-Mahi with Tamarillos and Wild Rice 98
Mango Raspberry Charlotte 120
Mango Raspberry Terrine 134
Mango Strudel 117
Marinated Peaches with Raspberry Sabayone 128
Melon Balls in Port Sauce 54
Monkfish Medallions with Eggplants and Coconut Sauce 101
Monkfish with Sliced Persimmon and Curry Sauce 92
Mussel Ragout with Lychees and Pink Grapefruit 95

Orange Carrot Soup 65

Passion Fruit Granita 132
Passion Fruit Sabayone 128
Pear Sorbet 130
Pears and Grapefruit Salad with Cooked Ham 50
Pickled Salmon with Grapefruit and Green Asparagus 52
Pike with Lime-Fennel Sauce and Star Fruit 90
Pomegranate Granita 133
Pork Chops in Plum Sauce 80
Pork Steak with Hazelnut Crust and Tamarillo Sauce 79

Prosciutto with Pears and Marinated Figs 56
Purified Sugar 47

Quince Chutney 75

Red Snapper with Fried Guavas and Curried Risotta 96
Red Snapper with Nashi Fritters and Ginger Sauce 97
Red Wine Pears 126
Roast Beef with Mustard Fruits 56
Rum-Flavored Plums with Two Kinds of Chocolate Mousse 125

Salmon Fillet with Cold Avocado and Watercress Sauce 88
Salmon Fillet with Rambutan Vinaigrette 61
Sesame Parfait with Kumquat Sauce 134
Shrimp in Saffron Dough with Cherimoya Sauce 104
Shrimp Kabobs with Mango Rice 104
Shrimp with Orange Noodles and Orange Sauce 103
Sirloin Steak with Spicy Mango Chutney 74
Sliced Raw Beef with Avocado and Olive Vinaigrette 58
Smoked Salmon Rosettes with Pomegranate Jelly and Mustard Sauce 52
Sole with Fruit Sauce 100
Spring Rolls with Papaya 57
Strawberry and Quince Cream Roll 118

Tamarillo Sorbet with Gin 130
Tamarillo Yogurt Roll 119
Tangerine Sorbet 130
Turkey Kabobs with Fruit 85
Turkey with Fig Beignets 85

Veal in Lemon Mangosteen Sauce 76
Veal Piccata in Mushroom Ragout with Nectarines 76

Apple
Hot Apple Soup 65
Little Nut Tarts with Mixed Fruit 110
Monkfish with Sliced Persimmon and
  Curry Sauce
Turkey Kabobs with Fruit 85

Apricot
Apricot Tart 117
Chicken Breast with Curried Fruits and
  Grated Coconut 68

Avocado
Avocado Buttermilk Soup with Salmon
  Cakes 61
Avocado Orange Salad with Raspberry
  Vinaigrette 50
Salmon Fillet with Cold Avocado and
  Watercress Sauce 88
Sliced Raw Beef with Avocado and
  Olive Vinaigrette 58

Banana
Bacon-Seasoned Pike with Banana-
  Peanut Butter Sauce 88
Banana Souffle with Chilled Cactus
  Pear Butter 138
Chicken Breast with Curried Fruits and
  Grated Coconut 68
Halibut Steak in Vegetable Sauce with
  Fried Fruit 98
Monkfish with Sliced Persimmon and
  Curry Sauce 92

Blueberry
Blueberry Cake with Royal 112

Cactus Pear
Banana Souffle with Chilled Cactus
  Pear Butter 138
Cod with Horseradish Crust and Cactus
  Pear Sauce 92

Cape Gooseberry
Little Fruit Tarts with Lemon Cream
  109
Turkey Kabobs with Fruit 85

Cherimoya
Flounder and Salmon Roulade with
  Cherimoya Sauce 91

Shrimp in Saffron Dough with
  Cherimoya Sauce 104
Sole with Fruit Sauce 100

Cherry
Cherry and Hazelnut Cake 114
Cherry Streusel 114

Coconut
Chicken in Spicy Coconut Sauce 69
Chicken Breast with Curried Fruits and
  Grated Coconut 68
Coconut Ginger Fancy Cake 110
Monkfish Medallions with Eggplants
  and Coconut Sauce 101

Cranberry
Emperor's Scrambled Pancake with
  Cranberries 136
Lamb Shanks in Cranberry Red Wine
  Sauce 80

Dates
Algerian Date Cake 112
Dates Filled with White Mocha Sauce
  with Pineapple Ice Cream 126
Lemon Muffins with Dates 108

Figs
Chicken Liver Pate with Fig Confit 59
Exotic Fruit Gratin 140
Prosciutto with Pears and Marinated
  Figs 55
Turkey with Fig Beignets 85

Grapefruit
Exotic Fruit Salad 124
Halibut Steak in Vegetable Sauce with
  Fried Fruit 98
Mussel Ragout with Lychees and Pink
  Grapefruit 95
Pears and Grapefruit Salad with Cooked
  Ham
Pickled Salmon with Grapefruit and
  Green Asparagus 52

Grapes
Little Nut Tarts with Mixed Fruit 110

Guava
Red Snapper with Fried Guavas and
  Curried Risotta 96

Kiwi
Exotic Fruit Salad 124
Exotic Fruit Gratin 140
Halibut Steak in Vegetable Sauce with
  Fried Fruit 98
Little Fruit Tarts with Lemon Cream
  109

Kumquats
Chicken with Kumquats 72
Sesame Parfait with Kumquat Sauce
  134

Lemon
Lemon Chicken 70
Lamb Curry in Lemon Sauce 83
Lemon Muffins with Dates 108
Lemon Soup 63
Little Fruit Tarts with Lemon Cream
  109
Veal in Lemon Mangosteen Sauce 76

Limes
Melon Balls in Port Sauce 54
Pike with Lime-Fennel Sauce and Star
  Fruit 90
Pomegranate Granita 133
Roast Beef with Mustard Fruits 56
Sole with Fruit Sauce 100

Loquat
Chicken Breast with Curried Fruits and
  Grated Coconut 68

Lychees
Chicken Breast with Curried Fruits and
  Grated Coconut 68
Mussel Ragout with Lychees and Pink
  Grapefruit 95
Salmon Fillet with Rambutan
  Vinaigrette 61

Mango
Exotic Fruit Gratin 140
Little Fruit Tarts with Lemon Cream
  109
Mango Raspberry Charlotte 120
Mango Raspberry Terrine 134
Mango Strudel 117
Roast Beef with Mustard Fruits 56
Sirloin Steak with Spicy Mango
  Chutney 74
Shrimp Kabobs with Mango Rice 104

Mangosteen
Exotic Fruit Gratin 140
Exotic Fruit Salad 124
Veal in Lemon Mangosteen Sauce 76

Melon
Creamed Melon Soup 62
Exotic Fruit Salad 124
Melon Balls in Port Sauce 54

Nashi
Red Snapper with Nashi Fritters and
    Ginger Sauce 97
Roast Beef with Mustard Fruits 56

Nectarine
Chicken with Nectarines and Scallions
    71
Veal Piccata in Mushroom Ragout with
    Nectarines 76

Orange
Avocado Orange Salad with Raspberry
    Vinaigrette 50
Exotic Fruit Salad 124
Lamb Medallions with Seville Orange
    Sauce 82
Orange Carrot Soup 65
Sesame Parfait with Kumquat Sauce
    134
Shrimp with Orange Noodles and
    Orange Sauce 103
Sole with Fruit Sauce 100

Papaya
Beef Tenderloin with Papaya and
    Ginger 73
Roast Beef with Mustard Fruits 56
Spring Rolls with Papaya 57

Passion Fruit
Chicken Breast with Curried Fruits and
    Grated Coconut 68
Passion Fruit Granita 130
Passion Fruit Sabayone 128

Peach
Halibut Steak in Vegetable Sauce with
    Fried Fruit 98
Marinated Peaches with Raspberry
    Sabayone 128

Pear
Pear Sorbet 130
Pears and Grapefruit Salad with Cooked
    Ham 50
Prosciutto with Pears and Marinated
    Figs 55
Red Wine Pears 126

Persimmon
Exotic Fruit Gratin 140
Monkfish with Sliced Persimmon and
    Curry Sauce 92

Pineapple
Cod with Pineapple 94
Dates Filled with White Mocha Sauce
    with Pineapple Ice Cream 126
Exotic Fruit Gratin 140
Ham Ragout with Pineapple 78
Turkey Kabobs with Fruit 85
Roast Beef with Mustard Fruits 56

Plum
Little Nut Tarts with Mixed Fruit 110
Pork Chops in Plum Sauce 80
Rum-Flavored Plums with Two Kinds of
    Chocolate Mousse 125

Pomegranate
Pomegranate Granita 133
Smoked Salmon Rosettes with
    Pomegranate Jelly and Mustard
    Sauce 52

Pomelo
Exotic Fruit Gratin 140

Quince
Quince Chutney 75
Strawberry and Quince Cream Roll 118

Rambutan
Chicken Breast with Curried Fruits and
    Grated Coconut 68
Salmon Fillet with Rambutan
    Vinaigrette 61

Raspberry
Mango Raspberry Charlotte 120
Mango Raspberry Terrine 134
Marinated Peaches with Raspberry
    Sabayone 128

Star Fruit
Pike with Lime-Fennel Sauce and Star
    Fruit 90
Roast Beef with Mustard Fruits 56

Strawberry
Chilled Strawberry Soup with Deep-
    Fried Strawberries 137
Strawberry and Quince Cream Roll 118

Tamarillo
Exotic Fruit Salad 124
Little Fruit Tarts with Lemon Cream
    109
Mahi-Mahi with Tamarillos and Wild
    Rice 98
Pork Steak with Hazelnut Crust and
    Tamarillo Sauce 79
Tamarillo Sorbet with Gin 130
Tamarillo Yogurt Roll 119

Tangerine
Calf's Tongue and Tangerine Salad with
    Lemon Balm Vinaigrette 50
Tangerine Sorbet 131